THE PATH TO ENLIGHTENMENT

Other titles in the Communities of Faith Series:

Submitting to God: Introducing Islam
Vivienne Stacey

A Way of Life: Introducing Hinduism
Ram Gidoomal and Robin Thomson

Communities of Faith

The Path to Enlightenment

Introducing Buddhism

John R. Davis

Hodder & Stoughton

LONDON SYDNEY AUCKLAND

British Library Cataloguing in Publication Data
A record for this book is available from the British Library

ISBN 0 340 69442 4

Typeset by Avon Dataset Ltd, Bidford-on-Avon, Warks

Printed and bound in Great Britain by
Clays Ltd. St Ives plc, Bungay, Suffolk

Hodder and Stoughton
A division of Hodder Headline PLC
338 Euston Road
London NW1 3BH

Contents

Series Editor's Preface   vii

Acknowledgments   ix

1   Where and How It All Started   1

2   Founders of the Faith and Early
Expansion   23

3   Sacred Texts and Serious Teachings   51

4   Chalk and Cheese or Just Two
Cheeses? A Comparison of Doctrines   69

5   Spirituality and Worship – Public
and Private Devotion   99

6   Ethics and Morality – Virtues and Vices   117

7   Leadership Structures and Religious
Offices   137

8   Propagating the Faith – The
Missionary Mandate of Buddhism   154

Suggestions for Further Reading   171

Index   174

Series Editor's Preface

There is a human tendency to try to present one's own beliefs, values and practices in a good light by deliberately presenting other beliefs, etc. in as bad a light as possible. In this series of books, the authors will not be guilty of misrepresentation, but will be guided by a basic Christian principle – that we should love our neighbours as we love ourselves. Therefore, the same respect and generosity will be given to each faith as Christians would wish for their own faith.

In this series on world faiths we are aiming to produce reference works which will be scholarly in terms of their accuracy and authority, completely fair to others, so that members of different faith communities will recognise themselves in the presentations, and also easily accessible to the general reader.

At the same time, they are written from a confident Christian perspective, and in each book the author will engage in a serious dialogue with the beliefs, values and practices of the faith which he/she is presenting. The authors all have genuine knowledge of the faith about which they are writing, personal experience of the community which holds that faith, a proven ability to reflect deeply on the issues involved, and the gift of being a good communicator. They are all practising Christians who are involved in dialogue with people of other faiths and cultures. Their interaction is sensitive and informed.

In each volume we shall explore a distinct faith and meet the community which lives by it. While the aim is to produce resources which capture the essential and timeless beliefs and values of each faith, full attention is given to the major contemporary issues and personalities. In the same way, while it is important to be aware of the global context of each faith, significant attention will be paid to the situation in the United Kingdom.

In order to make it easier to cross-reference among the books in this series, we have organised each book along the same lines. Topics dealt with in the numbered chapters will be the same in each book, no matter what the titles may be. You are therefore invited to join us in a great exploration of the world's faiths.

Buddhism is the world religion which probably more than any other confuses the typical Western person – especially someone brought up in the Christian faith. It has a rich tradition and a large and devoted following, but there is no 'God' at its heart – not at least as theists perceive of God. And yet the mysterious nature of the Buddhist faith is also a source of great fascination for many Westerners who have become disillusioned by excessive individualism and secularism. So what does lie at Buddhism's centre? John Davis takes us gently but confidently into the Buddhist world in this sensitive and accessible book.

Walter Riggans

Acknowledgments

I wish to express grateful thanks to my family for their patience during the period over which this book has been written. I am particularly thankful for the significant amount of time and energy my son Graham has given, not only to assiduous reading of the manuscript many times, but also in suggesting numerous important changes and corrections.

John R. Davis
Moorlands College, 1997

I

Where and How It All Started

Eastern mysticism has emerged as an engaging alternative to traditional Western belief systems in the post-war era. At the forefront of this burgeoning interest in oriental faiths is Buddhism, which has been quite widely adopted in the West and popularised by politicians and pop stars alike. Media inspired visions of barefooted saffron robed monks trailing casually in procession across paddy fields under the midday tropical sun; devotees placing offerings into begging bowls; fragrant incense swirling and wafting into the air around a fascinating looking shrine with devotees prostrate before a massive image of the Buddha; a solitary monk meditating in lotus position in the middle of a thick forest; these have all contributed to what could be interpreted as a superficial and unreal picture of what Buddhism is all about.

It is for this reason that the important question for our consideration is whether such fleeting, rather shallow perceptions really reflect what is at the core of this ancient belief system, or are there other deeper more mysterious and even more profound insights and truths about human life and nature, that we need to uncover?

The original Sanskrit meaning of the word for Buddha (*budh*) could give us a clue, for it means 'to awake' – 'to be enlightened'. The aim of this book is to escort the reader on an investigative trail, into a world hitherto virtually uncharted by the average Westerner; a journey of discovery, to find out for instance, what the Buddha really meant when he spoke of his own experience of 'enlightenment'.

This will be a journey that takes us down the ages, through the misty past, to engage in an almost impossible enterprise, of unravelling history from myth, fact from fiction and faith from fantasy. The journey is a long one – it takes us back nearly six hundred years before Christ to encounter this intriguing person – the Buddha.

There is no question that the Buddha was an important person, a contemporary of many other famous and infamous people. Among them were Pythagoras (Greece), Zoroaster (Iran/ Persia), Cyrus (Assyria) who, having captured Jerusalem, permitted the Old Testament Nehemiah to return in order to rebuild the temple and the walls of the ruined city.

While recognising the difficulty of our task, we will first of all try to untangle history[1] from the myths and legends that surrounded the Buddah[2] – 'the Enlightened One'. As Michael Pye indicates,

> This mythologisation means that the seeker of historical 'biography' is forced farther and farther back into complicated textual studies, making use of parallel writings in Sanskrit and Chinese, hoping that some clear touchstone for dividing fact will emerge. Alas no easy result has appeared. It seems sometimes that the more complicated the research is, the less probable are its results.[3]

From time to time we will be moving into areas of myth, legend and miracle that appear hardly credible to the Western rationalistic mind; but rather than dismiss all such occurrences as not having happened or as mere constructions of wishful thinking believers, it would be fairer to see them as refractions or reflections of some extraordinary teaching or event in the Buddha's life. If one looks at one's self in a 'hall of mirrors', on the one hand one sees grotesque distortions in the reflection, but on the other, the very fact that there are such distortions at all, proves or verifies one's existence.

The Buddha's family/clan name was Gautama (Sanskrit),

Gotoma (Pali) and his personal name was Siddhartha, which means 'he who has reached his goal'. He is sometimes addressed as Sakyamuni Gotama, indicating his family clan or tribe, the Sakyas. He was probably born in 563/566 BC in an area called Lumpini which straddles the borders of southern Nepal and Northern India – 230 kilometres north of Benares.

During this period, the whole of Asia had been experiencing an increasing time of unrest until it became overwhelmed by 'a tidal wave' of new religious belief systems. All sorts of religious gurus travelled far and wide espousing new philosophies and ideas that were eagerly accepted. Various movements began clashing with each other, vying for acceptance among the masses who were becoming increasingly disenchanted with their own religious beliefs. Many had reluctantly come to the conclusion that their own belief systems were morally bankrupt, because of widespread corruption. This among other things included making extortionate demands from poor people who could ill afford the requirements of expensive sacrifices which had to be offered for most 'transition-rite' ceremonies, such as birth, puberty, marriage and death. The poor were becoming poorer and the rich priest castes were becoming richer.

Among the more well known contemporary popular belief systems of the day, apart from Hinduism, were Confucianism, Shintoism, Taoism and of course Buddhism. In fact Confucius, Lao-tzu and the Buddha could all be classed as 'Protestants' in the literal meaning of the term, since each developed radical protest movements, which were reacting against the unreasonable demands of their own beliefs, such as the sacrificial systems and the elitist hierarchical structures of the day. They could be perceived as the Martin Luthers of their own time and generation who established their own reformation movements.

Popular tradition affirms that the Buddha came from a princely family and his father, Shuddhodanna, reigned over a princedom. However, the various texts could be interpreted to mean that he was governor of a province in the

kingdom of Kosala, rather than having 'royal blood'.
Whatever the case he came from an important prestigious
family that belonged to the *Sakiya* tribe and were of the
higher 'warrior caste' (*khattiya*).[4] The city of Kapilavatsu,
in the foothills of the Himalayas, was the stronghold of
the Sakiya tribe. It is said that while his mother was
travelling from this city to her parents' home in Devadaha
to give birth, on the way, in a grove of trees near Lumbini
village Gotama was born.

Political and religious turmoil seemed to entrap the
Shuddhodanna kingdom and many of the surrounding
lesser princedoms. The ever expanding powerful kingdom
of Magadha, from the north, appeared to be swallowing
these smaller kingdoms and there was a general feeling of
foreboding, unease and uncertainty in the air. At the same
time within Hinduism itself, there was growing dissatisfaction with the belief system propagated by the *Brahmin*
priests, the leaders of the Hindu religion. As indicated, this
centred on two particular areas. First, the increasing
demand for expensive sacrifices which could not be
afforded by the ordinary person and second, the anti-social
caste system that 'predestined' most people to the lower
castes including the 'out-castes' or 'untouchables'. The
elite, the especially privileged castes, included the very
people who controlled the sacrificial system, the Brahmin
priests. So, it was against this dark and confusing background that an almost insignificant light began to flicker –
the dawn of 'enlightenment' had begun.

The Buddha's Birth

Although Lumpini was where the Buddha was born, this
was not understood to be the beginning of his existence as
far as Buddhist teaching is concerned. He had already
experienced many rebirths stretching over millions of
years, experiencing previous existences as animals, men
and indeed gods. It was said that 'a hundred thousand
aeons ago', in a previous life, the Buddha met and was

inspired by a previous Buddha called Metteya, who would in a future period of human history return to become the saviour of the world.

Apart from some of the more conservative renditions of the Buddha's origins,[5] there is a massive collection of 550 'birth stories' surrounding the Buddha's origins and previous lives which are called the *Jataka*. It is in this book that his previous lives are recounted and he is recorded as having descended from heaven, with signs wonders and miracles accompanying his birth life and death.[6] His teaching was embellished with various reports of his ability to travel through the air. At least three visits to Sri Lanka by this means are reported (none historically recorded). His 'footprints' abound throughout South East Asia and even today some suddenly appear as contemporary imprints of his apparent more recent visits.

One of the more famous apocryphal stories is that the Buddha had been waiting in heaven for many aeons, for the auspicious time for his arrival on earth. He chose the right family, the right time and the right place to arrive,

> for his mother, he took the virtuous Maya, wife of Shuddhodanna who had shown her purity and excellence during previous existences in one hundred thousand ages of the world. One night, Maya, who had made a vow of chastity, dreamed that a white elephant entered her womb. Ten months later in the grove of Lumpini, on the day of the full moon in May, she bore the child. The earth trembled and supernatural beings were present at the birth; and Maya died seven days later, for she who gave birth to a Buddha may never serve any other purpose afterwards.[7]

Many of these stories are obviously fables, but they do add significance and meaning to who the Buddha was to become when he arrived at the palace as a baby. This birth was significant in that there had been a number of prophecies given to his father, that the boy would become either a great ruler or a wandering mendicant. It was reported that 108 Brahmins were invited to a special festival at the palace. On the day of Gotama's conception, seven Brahmins prophesied that one who had certain marks, wheels on the soles of his feet, and who was born into this family, would either become a powerful universal king or a poor wandering Buddha. However, an eighth Brahmin, a young man known from his clan as Kondanna, held up one finger and prophesied that his Buddhahood would be certain. The Brahmins then told the king that his son would leave the world after seeing the four signs – an old man, a sick man, a corpse and an ascetic. 'Accordingly guards were stationed at the four quarters to prevent these four from coming to the sight of his son.'[8]

Through fear of the latter prophecy being fulfilled, Gotama's father used every means to protect and shelter him from the outside world and its influences. So, as a boy he enjoyed a life of absolute luxury and ease, being cared for by his mother's sister Mahapatjapati. Gotama was thoroughly spoiled, and given the best education possible which, in keeping with tradition among the ancient Indian nobility, did not include learning to read and write! It did cover the arts, sciences and even physical education.

Gotama's religious education would have centred on his own family beliefs which were naturally Hindu, and he would have been thoroughly conversant with the famous Hindu Scriptures, the *Vedas*. No doubt, he imbibed the essence of Hinduism as a child, by singing some of the thousand or so hymns that make up the *Rig Veda*. As we learn by heart all sorts of 'fairy' stories, so Gotama would have known the epic stories of Hinduism such as the *Mahabharata*. From these stories and hymns he would certainly have drawn an understanding of the Hindu priesthood, the caste system, the continual interplay between human beings and the gods. All these would have been making a deep impression on his fertile mind. No doubt too, he would have come under the influence and power of the priesthood of that time which even at that stage he may have already been uneasy about, because after his enlightenment he immediately abandoned the values that lay behind both the power of the priesthood and the hierarchical nature of the caste system. It may have been that even at this impressionable age, Gotama, although enjoying the privileges of upper class living, could have begun to feel twinges of guilt because of his luxurious lifestyle. There is one record that reveals this sense of revulsion where it is written: 'He awoke to find his female musicians sleeping round him in disgusting attitudes. Then filled with loathing for his worldly life he made his decision, and ordered his charioteer Channa to saddle his horse Kanthaka.'[9]

Gotama may have been subtly introduced to other insights about life in spite of his father's protection, because one cannot delve far into any sacred literature without being confronted with the realities of life. 'In popular Hinduism the Rama story is not only heard from early childhood, but becomes the basis for everyday life. Rama will be invoked at the start of any undertaking and then thanked on its successful completion. His exploits become an example to follow and an encouragement to upright behaviour. His name will be used to *console* the aged and chanted by the assembled mourners, as the bodies of the dead are taken away for cremation.'[10]

At this stage, at least officially, Gotama should never have been allowed to be exposed to pain – so how could he understand why anyone would need *'consolation'*? He would certainly never have been allowed to join 'assembled mourners', or witness 'the bodies of dead people being taken away for cremation'. He should have been cocooned in a cosmetic unreal world, but within this fragile egg-shell existence, the cracks were already beginning to appear.

He married a girl called Yashodara when he was sixteen, and at the same time had a harem of other ladies, who anticipated his every bidding. A son Rahula was born when Gotama was twenty-nine years old. He recalls this period of his life later disdaining its reality. 'I was spoiled, very spoiled. I anointed myself only with Benares sandalwood and dressed only in Benares cloth. Day and night a white sunshade was held over me. I had a palace for the winter, one for the summer and one for the rainy season. In the four months of the rainy season I did not leave the palace at all, and was surrounded by female musicians.'[11]

It seemed Gotama lacked nothing in terms of physical pleasure or material possessions. Yet in the midst of all the luxurious indulgence, he was obviously seeking something which he did not possess – if that was possible. The name which Gotama gave to his son may have been an indication, even at this early stage, of his own growing dissatisfaction with his materialistic and egocentric lifestyle. Common to many other cultures, children were often given names that would reflect or symbolise a wish or an unexpressed desire of the father. Rahula means 'chain'. Despite having all that he ever wanted or needed, could it have been that he may have felt that he was 'chained' at this stage? Any lesser mortal would surely have opted for the *status quo* and enjoyed it. But this 'dis-ease' within triggered desires to know what really was on the other side of the palace walls. Palace walls that had been designed to protect him, but which now were perceived as prison bars to keep him from 'knowing' what life was really all about beyond the wall.

Beyond the Wall

Various fables surround Gotama's escapade beyond the walls of the palace grounds. The *Jataka* commentary introduces the 'other world' element to the story indicating that it was the gods that began to arouse Gotama's concern for the distressed, the diseased, and the dying. Some accounts seem to indicate that it was actually the gods themselves that appeared in these forms. The most common account seems to maintain that at the time of the full moon (June/ July) Gotama set out for his usual evening ride with his charioteer but on this particular occasion they went beyond the walls.

Another of the fables in the *Jataka* states that the gods muffled the sound of the hooves of his horse during the hasty exit while the city gate was opened by the god that dwelt there. Gotama discovered on the outside that which he had secretly feared. He met a man in the grip of a terrible disease, a wizened old man in the last stages of senility and the body of a dead man being carried by a group of mourners to be cremated. This cataclysmic event shattered Gotama's pretentious dreams and brought him face to face with the grim reality of what life was all about.

It was at this moment he determined to search for an answer to this meaningless suffering. Again this 'Aesop's fables'-style book, the *Jataka*, intertwines what was for all intents and purposes an historical experience of the Gotama, with all sorts of manifestations of the gods – good and bad. In response to turning away from all his past, the infamous *Mara*, the tempter, approached Gotama. Standing in the air, he exhorted him to return to his palace and extended to him the promise of even greater luxury with kingdoms and islands over which he would reign. From this time on, so the story goes, Mara became Gotama's close escort, shadowing him wherever he went, seeking to find some way of destroying him. Devotees claim that the existence of Buddhism is the proof that Gotama did not succumb to Mara's enticements. Another fable states that Gotama's horse, having supposedly listened to his conversation with the charioteer, and anticipating his master would no longer return to his palace, turned back toward home and died shortly of a broken heart. It was reported to have been immediately reborn a god! There is a famous Buddhist shrine called *Kanthakanivattana*, 'The Shrine of the turning back of Kanthaka' (the name of the horse). This is a real shrine, but the reason for its construction does not seem to be plausible.

The Renunciation

Gotama's reaction to what he saw on that afternoon was absolute. He immediately beat a hasty retreat from the palace, eastward into the depths of the forest for a period

and then went on to a small township known as Anipiyha.
Here he discarded his princely robes and was handed
yellow robes by one of the gods. He thereupon shaved his
head and renounced his past completely, including his
palaces, his riches, his wife and child and all his worldly
goods. A famous shrine was erected at this spot called
Kashayagrahana, 'The Taking of the Yellow Robes Shrine'.

Gotama had indulged in a life of luxury in the extreme,
he now began a life of austerity and asceticism to the
opposite extreme. He sought out two Hindu sages, famous
for their self-mastery and depth of perception and with
them he practised all sorts of meditation techniques,
including Yoga. For six years he left no stone unturned in
his desperate pursuit for some answer to the dilemma of
existence. As far as he could see at that time, there could
be no other way than the way of the Hindu gurus or
Brahmins. They continually strove to find solutions to the
meaninglessness of existence. They hoped, that through
fasting, self abnegation, and every form of meditation they
might achieve *Nirvana*, that final state of the extinction of
all desire. Gotama embraced these extremes with an eager-
ness that surpassed all his contemporaries in his zeal to
mortify the demands of the flesh. During one particular
period it was said that he fasted for forty-nine days. He
describes his own inner journey which was common with
the other aspirants.

I thought if I were to take food only in small amounts,
as much as my hollowed palm would hold, juice of
beans, vetches, chickpeas, or pulse . . . My body became
extremely lean. The mark of my seat was like a camel's
footprint through the little food. The bones of my spine
when bent and straightened out were like a row of
spindles through little food. When I thought I would
touch the skin of my stomach, I actually took hold of
my spine, and when I thought I would touch my spine I
took hold of the skin of my stomach, so much did the
skin of my stomach cling to my spine through little
food . . . then I thought those ascetics and Brahmins in

the past, who have suffered sudden, sharp, keen, severe pains, at the most have not suffered more than this. But by this severe mortification I do not attain superhuman truly noble knowledge and insight. Perhaps there is another way to enlightenment . . . but when I took solid food and gained strength then the five monks left me in disgust saying 'the ascetic Gotama has given up striving'.[12]

It is reported that Gotama went to such degrees of self-denial that he finally fell unconscious. News reached his father that he had died. Consequently, after nearly seven long years of fruitless searching together with five of his disciples, Gotama began seriously to question his own religious assumptions and belief system. If it is impossible to attain enlightenment through such absolute and total self-abnegation, could it be that there was another way? Whatever the case, for this most dedicated and sincere searcher for the truth, neither the way of luxury and indulgence in the palace on the one hand, nor extreme austerity and personal deprivation on the other, had led him nearer to an answer. Deeply unhappy with the results these polarised extremes had produced, he was now led to ask the question – was there some other way? Could there be an alternative answer to the mysteries of life and existence? Could there be a synthesis? Could there be 'a middle path'?

It was at this point that Gotama's five friends who were monks abandoned him in disgust, seeing evidence of his possible compromise away from the path of austerity. Now we find Gotama, in his emaciated state, hovering between life and death, sitting under the famous Bo tree. What must have been his feelings at this time? Did he fear he would have to experience even more cycles of reincarnation? This sense of foreboding and 'unknowing' must have weighed heavily on his frail body. Little did he realise that he was also on the verge of a new beginning.

It is evident that Gotama's 'enlightenment' derived from his own long struggle and inner spiritual journey. His new belief emanated from and was still in many respects closely related to his former beliefs in Hinduism. There is no doubt concerning his remarkable discoveries, and it would be interesting to compare his understanding and experience of what he now perceived as 'truth' with what a famous biblical religious leader, St Paul, experienced. He too had an 'enlightening' experience, he too was devout and zealous toward his own religion even before his 'experience'. By contrast, however, he made no claim to 'enlightenment' through austerity, self-mortification, pursuit of an inner spiritual journey, or even a 'middle way' like Gotama. Paul was, in fact, suddenly confronted with the sound of a voice from heaven. The very person who right up to that moment, he believed was a false prophet and who he hated so intensely, was now addressing him personally and audibly from heaven indicating that he was 'the Way the Truth and the Life'. Jesus Christ had revealed himself to Paul in such a way, that he too was transformed into one of the greatest leaders of what was also a new faith emerging from the old.

Under the Bo Tree – The Tree of 'Wisdom'

Many people seem to think that Gotama's 'enlightenment' happened like a flash of lightning from the sky. This is celebrated on the night of the full moon in the lunar month (April/May) *Vesakha*. In actual fact, although there are various reports of the time-span of his enlightenment, from a period of time of three days to four weeks, there does seem to be general agreement that his depth of understanding developed through a number of progressive stages.

During the first stage he began to deepen his level of concentration and through meditation focused on 'the chain of causation'. He began to pierce layer after layer of consciousness and to comprehend his own previous existences (over one hundred thousand of them!) which he describes in detail; these include many different animal forms as well as human. He also recalled ninety-one 'aeons' of time measuring the coming and going (cycles or reincarnations) of world systems.[13]

His second stage led him to discover the law governing the meaningless cycle of birth, death and rebirth (*samsara*). The law is called the *Dharma*. According to this law, every element of the universe, human, animal or mineral is subject to change and decay. Humans are merely a confluence or composition of five elements (*skandhas*) which are in a constant state of flux, always changing from one degree of decay to another. Here the Buddha moves away from the original Hindu idea of 'personhood' (*atman*) with each human being possessing a 'soul', so that a reincarnation for a Hindu would be rather a 'transmigration' of the soul. But the Buddha saw no particular continuity of 'personhood' between one reincarnation and another – the only element that continues is the *karma* of a previous existence. The new being is totally independent from the previous one except that karma (good or bad) has somehow been transmitted between the two. Karma can be defined in terms of 'merit' gained or lost in a previous existence which impinges upon and is transferred to a present existence. These concepts will be defined and clarified in another chapter.

The third stage led Gotama to discover the 'Four Noble Truths':

1. The knowledge/fact of suffering
2. The source of suffering
3. The removal of suffering
4. The way to the removal of suffering (the Eightfold Path)

This was it. Here, encapsulated in a few sentences, is the very foundation of Buddhist teaching. While these stages were developing, we are told that there were all sorts of heavenly visitations and manifestations from thunderbolts to flashes of lightning. Accompanying this, legions of angels and armies of demons were conflicting with each other attempting either to protect or to destroy the one who was now to be called 'The Buddha'.

This cataclysmic event was accompanied by earthquakes and a massive battle with Mara (Satan) and his host of demons. The whole of Asia is full of pictorial and terracotta depictions of the Buddha's temptation and battle with the enemy. Mara and his host had failed in their numerous attempts to distract Gotama from his attaining enlightenment. Tradition has it that because of his accumulated merit Gotama was able to throw off the various intimidations and temptations launched at him by Mara and his demons. It is said that as a last ditch effort to defeat Gotama, Mara sent his three daughters, Discontent, Delight and Desire to seduce him, but he remained impervious to their advances so that finally Mara gave up, realising he had met not only his equal, but one who could not be contaminated by all of the attractions of 'the world, the flesh and the devil'. The story goes that while Gotama was struggling with these temptations, a massive seven-headed king cobra coiled itself round his body and spread its hood over his head so that he would be protected – the king of the serpents stayed there until the roaring elements of wind and rain had passed and there was peace. This is why the Buddha is so often depicted in images and pictures as sitting on top of a coiled serpent. It is interesting to contrast the imagery of the protector Serpent in Buddhism, and Satan the serpent-cum-arch-deceiver in the Bible.

It was almost immediately after his enlightenment that the Buddha wanted to preach his first sermon. But where was his congregation? He departed from the Bo tree and intuitively made his way to Benares to the now famous deer park, where he met the five ascetics who had previously deserted him. The *Jataka* stories record the Buddha's journey to Benares. It was said that having no money to pay the ferryman at the River Ganges, the Buddha crossed through the air. The ferryman was so impressed, from that time forward he abolished the ferry tolls for all ascetics!

On seeing Gotama in the distance, the five monks

decided at first to snub him because they saw him as a spiritual failure, one who had compromised his vows. However, as he approached nearer they were attracted by the change that had obviously taken place. They now became his first reluctant audience, and upon listening to what they perceived to be pearls of wisdom falling from his lips, the five became his first converts. The substance of this first sermon was to become the foundation for all the Buddha's subsequent messages which he continued to preach for forty-four years with missionary fervour, travelling far and wide across the vast Continent of India.

Before we eavesdrop on the Buddha's first message to his meagre audience, it is necessary to define the term 'enlightenment', in terms of Buddhist understanding. It is clear that the word does not extend to 'knowing every-thing' in terms of scientific knowledge, general knowledge, or even intellectual understanding as recognised from a Western perspective. Enlightenment here is a special mystic intuitive knowledge that reaches beyond the rational, beyond the empirical and beyond the limits of conscious intellectual exercise. It 'discovers' specific answers, but obviously not all answers. It refuses, for instance, to attempt to explain phenomena that may be unexplainable in terms of 'supernatural beings'. It rejects the whole idea or concept of there being a 'God' either as a Creator or Saviour. In its original pure form, it is essentially a-theistic. The Buddha made no claim to any special divine revelation or influence outside of himself. His teaching implies that if one goes as far as to say there was an 'originator' (intelligence?) behind this bewildering state of affairs called the cosmos, then whoever it was who created such a mess should be given the name 'Ignorance' (*avija*) – for who, with a grain of intelligence, would produce such an endless round of sickness, sorrow, suffering and sadness?

It therefore concludes, there is no God, no Creator, it offers no answers concerning the origins of the universe, for it does not seek them – it is looking for cure rather than cause. It is primarily concerned with the *fact* of suffering, its *effects*, and how to resolve the problem of endless cycles of existence. Enlightenment is therefore to be perceived as a special intuitive religious knowledge derived from Gotama's own personal experiences and perceptions, based upon his own reactions to the indulgence of excessive extravagance during his youth on the one hand and subsequent extreme self-mortification on the other. It seemed that the Buddha had discovered the only alternative. He had already poured his energies into both extremes – there could only be one way left and he called it 'the middle way'.

There were of course a number of other factors which inevitably impinged upon his understanding of enlightenment. They would have included his instinctive reactions against the corrupt caste system of the day; his disapproval of the requirements of the costly sacrificial systems which were keeping the poor very poor and the Brahmins very rich. Buddhism immediately strips away all class distinctions based on birth, cultural or economic considerations.

Added to this must have been the virtual desperation to find some way of deliverance or release from the endless cycle of reincarnations. Therefore implicit within the enlightenment process there must be some hope for the future (*Nirvana*), which by definition would be 'release' from all attachments of this world.

Another major factor must have been the Buddha's conviction that since he discovered this enlightenment by his own self-effort, and others had not found it by any other means, then logically it could only be attained by others in the same way – their own self-effort.

It is quite clear to all commentators of Buddhist teaching that the overarching motif or theme on that first day and for the rest of his life was centred on the importance of this self-effort. Some of his first recorded words to his group of listeners as he preached his first sermon called the 'Discourse setting in motion the wheel of truth' (*Dhrmacakrapravaratana sutra*) were:

Therefore be ye lamps unto yourselves. Rely on yourselves, and do not rely on external help . . . hold fast to the truth as a lamp. Seek salvation alone in the truth. Look not for assistance to anyone beside yourselves. Those who, either now or after I am dead, shall be a lamp unto themselves relying upon themselves only and not relying upon any external help, but holding fast to the truth as their lamp and seeking their salvation in the truth alone, not looking for assistance to anyone besides themselves, it is they Ananda, among my Bhikkhus (disciples) who shall reach the very topmost height![14]

We will expand on the content of this teaching in detail in Chapter 5. This emphasis on self-effort is in stark contrast to Christianity and to what Jesus Christ stated both concerning himself and his followers. He pointed to himself as 'The Light of the World', (the 'One who enlightens everyone who comes into the world'). He went on to say time and again throughout his teaching 'Without me you can do nothing.' So rather than self-effort, Christ indicated that human beings need to depend upon him for his power and strength for his forgiveness and purity. This concept of someone else being a 'saviour' does develop in later expression of Buddhism (*Mahayana*), where the *Bodhisattva* becomes the person who voluntarily suspends his release to Nirvana in order to assist those in need. In fact the future Buddha who is prophesied as the one who is to come to deliver the world, is certainly described as a 'saviour'; the *Metteya* could be translated as 'the One who extends mercy' or, 'The Prince of Peace/Mercy'. Of particular interest is the fact that certain ancient manuscripts of Buddhist Scripture and oral tradition from Cambodia, Thailand, Laos and Myanmar all indicate a common prophecy, that following the Buddha, there would be at the end of the age, a Messiah-like figure called the 'Prince of Peace/Mercy' who would bring salvation and light. An Indian source of Buddhism states that this person is to be the one who will take on human form to deliver the world. This source states that at the scene of his death, the Buddha made the following statement:

I am not the first Buddha who came upon earth, nor shall I be the last. In due time another Buddha will arise in this world, a holy one, a supremely enlightened one, endowed with wisdom in conduct, auspicious, knowing the universe, an incomparable leader of men, a master of angels and mortals. He will proclaim a religious life, wholly perfect and pure; such as I now proclaim . . . He will be known as Metteya, which means, he whose name is kindness.[15]

A further quotation from a dictionary of Buddhism indicates the following prophecy of a future Messiah:

I shall lift human beings out of the mire of gross ignorance and error, and enable them to cross over this troubled world to the realm of happiness on the farther shore. Those who are entangled in the meshes of sinful passions, or who still drink the bitter waters of unrighteous desires, or have lost their way in the endless maze of this troubled series of existences; to them shall I preach revealing to them the road to the pearly city, that is the Land of Happiness, Nirvana – I shall open with the key of true doctrine. With eye medicine shall I cleanse the eyes, that is the understanding of those whose vision is defective having become blurred by evil desire, or by anger, or hatred or ignorance . . . to those who have lost their way in the wilderness because of darkness I shall give you light.[16]

Another quite sensational find relates to an ancient manuscript discovered in a temple in Chiengmai in North Thailand, written in the language of the old kingdom, before Christian missionaries ever went to that country. It records a conversation the Buddha had with a Brahmin who asked him how he could be saved from the power of sin in his life. The Buddha is reported to have replied:

Regardless how many laws you may have kept, or even if you pray five times a day, you shall not be saved. A sin is too great to be washed away; even though I become a hermit for more than eight '*A-song-kai*' . . . The Brahmin asked what Metteya's character is. The Buddha replied that 'in his hands and feet are wounds, his side has a wound which was pierced and his forehead is full of scars from wounds. He is the gold ship to carry you to heaven where you will find the Tri-pra (the crystal Triune god). Thus give up following the old way. A spirit from heaven will come and dwell in your heart by which you will overcome your enemies for both four and eight directions.'[17]

Is it any wonder that when missionaries discovered this prophecy, they made claim (in spite of protest from Buddhist authorities) to the fact that this was indeed a very clear reference to the Lord Jesus Christ who was to come 600 years later.

As indicated elsewhere, the Buddha continued to share his 'Gems' of *Dharma* for forty-five years with whoever would listen. Then at the age of 80 while on yet another tour, he reached the home of a goldsmith, developed food poisoning and died.

Unanswered questions remain, especially concerning the nature of good or bad karma. To die of food poisoning – that is bad karma indeed. How could the Enlightened One be the victim of his own bad karma? How could he deserve this? Legend has it that as with his coming into the world, the cosmic forces erupted, with earthquakes and fire, so with his demise 'all heaven was let loose'. The Buddha's mortal remains were cremated, and the ashes (some of which we are told turned into diamonds or precious gems), were enshrined in a number of *stupas* as relics, and shared among devotees who took them to other places in the world where they were incarcerated in monuments.

1. Thomas states that St Jerome refers to 'a virgin gave birth from her side to Buddha, the chief person of their teaching,' but Thomas indicates that this was confused myth rather than history. Marco Polo clearly confirms his knowledge

about the Buddha, giving him his Mongolian title Sagamoni Barcan. He describes him as the son of the King of Ceylon and the first idol-founder, though he knew of his greatness as a moral teacher and declared that if he had been a Christian, he would have been a great saint of our Lord Jesus Christ, so good and pure was the life he led (Book III, ch. 15, p. 138). See Edward Thomas, *The Life of Buddha as Legend and History* (Routledge & Kegan Paul, 1975), p. xiv.

Christmas Humphries states: 'No biography was written for several hundred years after the Life had ended and the available sources for such information are such a mixture of history and legend as to prove the despair of all historians . . . as the centuries rolled by each version of the Life acquired an increasing garland of fabulous adventure, miracle and heavenly assistance. But legend is often a poetic form of history.' See *Buddhism* (Penguin Books, 1951), pp. 30–33.

2. H. W. Schumann states: 'The canonical Pali scriptures supply reliable information about the later years of Gotama's life. However, what we know of his youth stems from later texts and commentaries, from whose tangled mass of legends the historical kernel must be separated.' See *Buddhism* (Rider & Co., 1973), p. 17.

3. See Michael Pye, *The Buddha* (Duckworth, 1979), p. 6.

4. Pye states: 'It is usual to fix the dates of the Buddha's life by their relation to the much later accession of King Asoka to the throne of the kingdom of Maghada in 286 BC. King Asoka belonged to the Maurya dynasty. His grandfather, Canragupta is the first king who can be located in the chronology of general history, by his relations with the Greek Seleucid dynasty. Chanragupta won a military campaign against Seleucius Nikatork gaining territory on the river Indus in the north west of the Indian sub-continent. Peaceful exchanges also took place. This ancient contact between Greek and Indian civilisations should not be considered a matter of surprise. After all, they both shared a common ancestry of language and of mythology. Indian (Vedic), Persian and Greek polytheism all belong to the same

family. The grandson Asoka also exchanged missions with rulers of the Hellenistic world such as Antiochus II of Syria (260–246 BC) and Ptolemy II of Egypt (285–247 BC).' (*The Buddha*, p. 11)

5. These can be found in the Pali Scriptures of Theravada Buddhism, particularly three accounts in 'The Discourse of the Noble Quest' (*ariyapariyesana Sutta*), 'The Greater Discourse' (*Mahasaccaka Sutta*) and the first of the *Mahavagga*. In the first discourse there are no references to the Buddha's enlightenment under a Bo tree – just that he was seated in a pleasant place – nor is there any record of his struggle with the demon Mara which is made much of in other Scriptures.

6. One of the most famous fables concerning the Buddha's birth, recorded in art, on canvas and in prose, tells how 'A white elephant seemed to enter her body, and without causing her any pain, Maya, queen of that god-like king, bore in her womb the glory of his dynasty. But she remained free from the fatigues, depression and fancies which usually accompany pregnancies. Pure herself, she longed to withdraw into the pure forest in the loneliness of which she could practise trance ... when the queen noticed her time of delivery was approaching, she went to a couch over spread with an awning, thousands of waiting women looking on with joy in their hearts ... His birth was miraculous, so he issued from the womb as befits a Buddha. He did not enter the world in the usual manner, and he appeared like one descending from the sky and since he had for many aeons been in the practice of meditation, he was now born in full awareness, and not thoughtless and bewildered as other people are.' See E. Conze (ed.), *Buddhist Scriptures* (Penguin Classics, 1969), p. 35.

7. W. Metz, *A Lion Handbook: The World's Religions* (Lion Publishing, 1982), p. 222.

8. Thomas, *The Life of Buddha*, p. 44.

9. Ibid., p. 54.

10. Raymond Hammer, *Japan's Religious Ferment* (SCM Press, 1961), p. 181.

11. Ibid., p. 223.

12. Thomas, *The Life of Buddha*, pp. 64–66.
13. Peter Harvey, *An Introduction to Buddhism* (Cambridge University Press, 1990), p. 85.
14. Ann Bancroft, *Religions of the East* (Heinemann, 1974), p. 80.
15. See P. Carus, *The Gospel of Buddha* (New Delhi Book Trust, 1975), p. 196.
16. *A Dictionary of Buddhism: Chinese-Sanskrit-English-Thai* (Bangkok Press, 1976), p. 511.
17. J. Davis, *Poles Apart* (ATA Books, Bangkok, 1993), p. 119.

2

Founders of the Faith and Early Expansion

Among those renowned in Buddhism for their commitment to the Buddha and his teaching were members of his own family – his father and former wife became lay-followers; his son Rahula, his half-brother Nanda and some distant relatives like Anuruddha, Bhaddiya, all became his devout disciples. After prolonged consideration he granted his foster mother Mahapatjapati (who had persistently made appeals to him) permission to become a nun and to found an order of nuns. This order became defunct for a period, but was subsequently restored and is still in operation in many countries today. One of his earliest and most important disciples, his nephew and close companion, was called Ananda. He stayed with the Buddha for twenty-five years as his attendant and constant companion throughout his itinerant preaching journeys and was with him when he died at the age of 80, in 483 BC.

Many other influential people joined the small band, some of them well known for their distinctive activities. Sariputta was renowned for his wisdom and intellect, while Moggallana possessed magical powers; others were known for the extent to which they went in terms of severe asceticism or prolonged meditation. Then gradually a small army of devout lay people attached themselves to the Buddha. A certain King Bimbisara of Magadha commissioned a monastery to be built for the Buddha who dwelt there for a number of rainy seasons. So ex-prince Buddha became a friend to kings and people from high society who encouraged with missionary zeal, the spread of his teachings.

At the same time, as with leaders of other religions, enemies began to emerge who, like Judas Iscariot, were prepared to betray their leader. The Buddha was accused of all manner of heresy and corrupt teaching that, his opponents charged, would destroy the very structure of society. It was said he deliberately encouraged childlessness, celibacy, widowhood and the breaking up of families. He was even betrayed by members of his own household who plotted to murder him. At least three attempts were made on his life. In the first instance, a soldier was persuaded by Devadatta, a relative who had previously been a disciple, to murder the Buddha because he refused to hand over the leadership of the new order to him, but when the soldier drew near to the Teacher, he fell at his feet, confessed his guilt and made his vows to be a disciple. It was reported that there was a second attempt on his life by stoning, and although the Buddha did suffer minor injuries as a result, he was bravely undeterred in his mission of mercy. A third attempt on his life occurred when a wild elephant was deliberately let loose crashing into his pathway. It was said that the Buddha radiated such mercy towards the animal that it became tranquil immediately and ambled meekly on its way.

On his early travels the Buddha occasionally met various groups of Hindu Brahmins or gurus. Two groups of importance were the followers of Uru Kassapa (a matted-hair ascetic) who had 300 disciples, and those of his brother Gaya Kassapa who had 200 disciples. The story of their mass 'conversion' to Buddhism is quite astonishing as it is related in the *Jataka*. The Buddha is purported to have displayed his miraculous powers by overcoming two fictitious beasts (dragons) called 'Nagas' which vomited smoke and fire. He demonstrated telepathic powers by reading the thoughts of these brothers, split wood miraculously, created stoves for them to be warmed after bathing, and in all, is reported to have worked 3500 miracles. These demonstrations resulted in mass conversions when all who heard shaved their hair, dressed in saffron robes and repeated the three-fold formula necessary for ordination as followers of the Buddha – 'I take refuge in the Buddha, the *Dharma* (doctrine) and the Sangha (the order).'

Another famous story is told of a courtier of Prince Suhodhanna who was born on the same day as the Buddha. When the prince heard that the Buddha was in the district, he sent the courtier together with 1000 soldiers, inviting the Buddha to the palace to preach and teach. As the soldiers approached the Buddha, they were so overwhelmed that they turned *en masse* to him, forgetting their mission. A second courtier with another 1000 men was sent with the same result – this happened nine times! Finally the message got through and the Buddha now with as many as twenty thousand Arahats (followers) proceeded to the palace, where he was warmly welcomed and won the favour of the King and his household.

It became the custom for the Buddha and his followers to rise at dawn and to walk barefoot from house to house with begging bowls anticipating a generous response from the community. His disciples received their food with no acknowledgment of thanks to the donors – for it was understood that the givers themselves would be thankful that, through this act, they had been given the opportunity of accruing a considerable amount of merit which would be credited to their 'merit account' for the future. Such almsgiving is regarded as a long-term investment, for it would create the right karma that would in turn assure the giver of gaining a higher form of existence in their next reincarnation.

It was about this time that the Buddha returned to his own home to visit his father, wife and children. When his wife approached him, she bowed down before him, placed his feet on her prostrate shoulders and his father then gave account to the Buddha his son-in-law as follows:

Lord, my daughter, when she heard you were wearing yellow robes; put on yellow robes, when she heard you ate one meal a day, she herself took one meal; when she knew you had given up a large bed, she lay on a narrow couch; and when she knew you had given up garlands and scents, she too gave them up.[1]

With regard to these miraculous events, it has always been difficult to separate what was obviously myth or legend from what happened historically. Commentators do not agree on many points, but those who, while accepting the doctrines of Buddhism, perceive events from a naturalistic point of view, would relegate most of the so-called miracles and supernatural events to the creative imagination of his followers in their desire to adulate, elevate or glorify the Buddha to more than a mere human being. The Buddha would certainly have rejected such high estimation or deification of himself. As with all stories and legends, there are some that became favourites and the 'miracle of the pairs' is one of those particular stories that raises the Buddha far above the capabilities of ordinary human beings.

It happened when at first many of the Buddha's own family were not prepared to recognise him – the Buddha thereupon rose up into the air and flames of fire came from the upper part of his body, while streams of water poured out from his lower part. This process developed until fire came from the right side of the Buddha and water from the left side – this happened twenty-two times – he then created various illusions such as walking along a jewelled promenade in the sky. The *Jataka* reports that the Buddha performed this special 'miracle of the pairs' on at least three separate occasions. Such phenomenal activities are purported to have accompanied the Buddha's teaching wherever he went and as each year of his ministry passed, the records reflect an increasing extravagance of supernatural manifestations. Of course these miracles have no means of authentication or historical verification.

It is probable that the Buddha's teachings had far more profound effect than all the supposed miracles that he was reported to have performed. His teaching began to undermine the credibility of Hinduism (especially the crippling caste system), and contributed towards breaking its hold on the masses. He refused to be drawn into questions of the origins of humankind or the universe which were the endless/useless debates of the Hindu gurus. He would respond by asking what difference would *any* answer to such questions make, in terms of living a holy life? A certain monk said he would not follow the Buddha until he answered these fundamental questions, to which he replied in parable form:

'Suppose a man had been shot with an arrow and refused to have the arrow taken out of his body until he had discovered, what kind of bow it was that shot the arrow, and what was the name and family of the one who shot the arrow?' Buddha replied simply – 'that man would die without knowing these things! Even so if any one says "I will not follow the holy life under the Blessed One until he answers these questions, such as whether the Universe is eternal or not" – he would die with these questions unanswered.'[2]

For forty-five years the Buddha's itinerant ministry spread across the whole of North East India. As his teaching and fame spread there needed to be some type of structure or organisation to support and maintain the many thousands of people who were joining the movement. An order of monks was established called the 'Sangha' (see Chapter 8 for more details). Those who were formally ordained into the order took upon themselves vows of poverty and chastity. A special ordination ceremony would be part of the induction and the ordinand would have his head and eyebrows shaved. Then he would discard his ordinary attire and wear a long yellow saffron robe. For mendicant monks, the sum total of all their worldly goods could be carried around with them wherever they went and could be stored within the circumference of an open umbrella. In return for their austere lifestyle and their preaching, the monks would receive offerings of food from the faithful.

They would, however, only eat at the most two meals – one at dawn and the other no later than noon.

As he came toward the end of his life the Buddha became ill and called his faithful follower Ananda, indicating he would die within three months. Trying to console his grief the Buddha said:

> 'But now Ananda, have I not formerly declared to you that it is in the very nature of all things near and dear to us to pass away? How then Ananda seeing that whatever is brought into being contains within itself the inherent necessity of dissolution, how can it be that such a being (as the visible Gotama) should not be dissolved?' Shortly after this he addressed all his Disciples 'O Bhikkhus, I exhort you, saying all component things must grow old. Work out your own salvation.'[3]

Following these last words Buddha managed to walk to a Mango Grove at Cunda. A local blacksmith (some say goldsmith) prepared a meal for him, and it is recorded that a few days later the Buddha died from food poisoning as a result of this meal. Following his cremation, it was said that his ashes were shared among ten princes or rajahs who were rulers over the areas he traversed during his lifetime of travels. Ten *stupas* (monuments) were erected in which his ashes were interred. Today there is a cult following of pilgrims who come from all directions to 'worship' the relics at two of the most well-known *stupas*; one at the site of his enlightenment and the other in the deer park near Benares, the site of the Buddha's 'setting in motion the Wheel of Law' (see Chapter 8 for further details of places of pilgrimage). The extraordinary events purported to have happened surrounding the death of the Buddha are as sensational as those that occurred when he was born.

The inexplicable events surrounding the story do not end there, for an even more bizarre episode occurred in the middle of the nineteenth century. Some devotees discovered that one of the sacred *stupas* at Sanchi had been totally ransacked and the sacred contents mysteriously taken away. Many years after their disappearance, they eventually 'emerged' in a most unusual place – they had been secretly brought to the Victoria and Albert Museum in London where they were boldly on display! Subsequently, in the 1940s, following considerable protest from the Buddhist community worldwide, the 'relics' were returned to India with all the pomp and ceremony of a coronation to be laid at rest once again in the *stupa* at Sanchi.

Following the death of Gotama his closest disciples (tradition says there were sixty-one Arahats) came together as the founder members of what became known as the Sangha, to live in community and establish his teaching in a formal coherent manner. The Sangha developed into four sections. The first two included those 'professional' or full-time monks and nuns who took upon themselves vows of celibacy and chastity; the second two sections included male and female lay persons, who, while living ordinary lives within their own village communities, nevertheless laid claim to (or to be more precise, 'took refuge in') the 'Three Gems' and made appropriate vows (see details about the Sangha in Chapter 8).

The First Council of Rajagha: July/August 483 BC

By this time, about five hundred Arahats with the King's patronage held their first conference at Rajagha under the leadership of a certain Maha Kassapa. The outcome was the preliminary formation of the canon – at this time the doctrines were only in the form of 'oral tradition' with various monks being responsible for remembering and reciting the Buddha's teaching. The Buddha's follower Ananda was recognised as especially important for this council because of his constant companionship with the Buddha. He would have been able to recollect much of the oral teaching. Tradition says Ananda was able to recite all the teaching in the first and second basket of The Gems. Tradition also implies that Ananda's role at this council was very controversial in that contrary to what the Buddha had specifically stated, he advocated that women should be given full recognition to join the Sangha. The Buddha is reported to have stated that if and when women were allowed, the demise of the *Dharma* would arrive 500 years early! The Buddha was finally agreeable for there to be a women's order, but with a major caveat that left no one in any doubt that women *were* subservient to men.

Two of his restrictions were: 'A nun must always greet a monk with deference, rising from her seat and showing respect.' (It is nowhere indicated that there was a reciprocal rule for men.) And, 'A nun cannot give admonition or advice to a monk.' It must be said that most of the rules were formulated in order to protect nuns from possible dangers, and ensure they lived according to appropriate cultural *mores* of the time. While there are some differences of opinion as to whether it is necessary for women to be reincarnated into men before they can attain enlightenment and be released into Nirvana, it is reported that towards the end of his life, the Buddha affirmed that women could be enlightened instantly. He stated:

Not merely a hundred, nor two, nor three, four or five hundred, but far more are those nuns, my disciples, who by the elimination of defilements have here and now realised by direct knowledge the freedom of mind and wisdom that is without defilements, and who abide (in that realisation).[4]

This statement has been interpreted in different ways, thus the ambiguity of the conclusions that have been drawn from it (see Chapter 9 for further information about the importance of women's activities within Buddhism).

It was while the Rajagha Council was in progress that another contingent of 500 other monks were reported to have arrived with the claim that their leader, a mendicant monk called Purana, had memorised all of the Buddha's teaching. Upon invitation to recite, he declined and he and his followers went on their way independently to set up an alternative school, thus undermining the council's attempt to maintain unity among all the followers of the Buddha.

The Second Council of Vesali: 383 BC

One hundred years passed before a second formal gathering was convened which was called the Council of Vesali (both councils being named after the place where they met). This council, with 700 monks in attendance, convened with a view to solving the question of revising and moderating certain rules of conduct which appeared to be a liberalisation of what the Buddha had taught, but were now being raised by some of the monks. The suggestion of either revising or moderating was unacceptable to the conservative group. The result was that the order split in two and the council condemned the proposed revisions. The group who wanted a more liberal interpretation of doctrine and regulations formed the *Mahasanghikas*, 'Members of the Great Sangha', sometimes called 'the Greater Vehicle'. The conservatives were duly named the *Theravadins* 'Adherents of the Teaching of the Elders', sometimes called 'the Lesser Vehicle'. Although there were some disputable issues concerning the nature of rigorous or slackened discipline, the main controversy at this time centred on the nature of 'selfhood', what really constitutes 'personhood'. One school, called the *Puggalavadins*, insisted on the existence of personhood (*Puggala*), while the other argued for the concept of *anatta* 'no personhood'. The former school split into various factions and had a relatively strong following across India, perhaps because it approximated to the Hindu view. The importance of this division regarding doctrine lay in the proposition that if one maintained a belief in 'non-selfhood', then what appears to be 'a person' would merely be the temporary coming together of five elements (*skandhas*) and nothing of the 'person' could be transmitted from one reincarnation to another except karma. However, if one held to the former belief, then 'selfhood' implied the existence of a

real person – and if that be the case, then the 'transmigration of souls' (personhood) from one being to another
would be possible. For a detailed discussion, see Chapter
4.

The Third Council of Pataliputta: 253 BC

This was historically one of the most important councils.
By this time Buddhism in India had been splintering left,
right and centre, into smaller factions each with its own
particular emphasis or interpretation of the Buddha's
teachings. Some of the distinctive elements of Buddhist
teaching were being merged with various surrounding
philosophies and belief systems while other teaching, containing new elements of doctrine, began to emerge. Among
some groups, there developed a particular syncretistic
emphasis which sought close continuity with Hinduism,
so that the Buddha was regarded by them as the ninth
incarnation of the Hindu god Vishnu. This deification of
the Buddha contradicts much of his own teaching about
himself. He never claimed deity, he pointed the way of
salvation (for the few who attained), to the *Dharma* (the
teaching) rather than to himself. The principal cause of
this elevation of the Buddha arose from one of the most
famous volumes of Buddhist literature, the *Lotus Sutra*.
This was composed between the second century BC and
the second century AD. Edward Rice gives an insight into
its character:

> The work stresses the eternal Buddha-principle, repre-
> sented in innumerable forms to work out the salvation
> of all suffering humanity. In the *Lotus Sutra*, Buddha is
> the eternal omniscient, omnipotent, omnipresent;
> creator-destroyer, recreator of all worlds – concepts
> borrowed from Hinduism and carried over into
> Mahayana Buddhism. Its central thesis is that of
> universal salvation. Everyone and everything have
> within them the potentiality of Buddhahood.[5]

*

Considerable time and energy was spent in this council trying to clarify unresolved doctrinal matters from the last council, again centred on the nature of 'selfhood' or 'non-selfhood'. There seemed to be a preoccupation with 'dotting all the "i"s and crossing all the "t"s'. This third council/synod was convened by the renowned Emperor Asoka, a devout and zealous follower of the Buddha's teaching, and presided over by his brother Moggali-puttatissa, a distinguished monk.

King Asoka is reported to have begun his reign about 269 BC and continued for twenty-four years until one year after the death of Alexander the Great (322 BC). The impact of this king's influence cannot be underestimated. It has been said that he was the greatest ruler of India, his kingdom stretched from Afghanistan and Kashmir to the Bay of Bengal, from the foothills of the Himalayas to south of Bangalore. He was a mighty warrior and brutally subdued all hostilities from minor kingdoms until the whole of India was completely under his rule. Later, following his conversion, he became a lover of righteousness and the rule of justice. Some historians interpret some of Asoka's own teaching to be different from the *Dharma* in emphasis. He is considered to have developed some strong ideas of his own especially an almost 'universalistic' emphasis that salvation was available for all people in all religions as long as they were devout. The Buddha himself did not teach this because he saw 'the middle way' as the way of salvation in contradistinction from his previously held Hindu beliefs. King Asoka became the Defender of all Faiths. Certain rock inscriptions, attributed to have been written about him, record that he became deeply repentant for his part in brutality and felt strongly the guilt of his responsibility for murderous mass killings during his exploits, involving many thousands of innocent women and children. The rest of his life was dedicated to reversing the evils that he had committed.

It is recorded that he built 84,000 monasteries through-out his kingdom, in order to be commensurate with the

84,000 sections in the *Dharma*. He had a missionary heart and commissioned ambassadors of the *Dharma* to the Tamils of South India, to Syria, Macedonia, Egypt, Cyrene, Cyprus and Ceylon.

Many decisions and developments occurred during this council with the aim of resolving the differences between the various schools of thought. Over one thousand monks came together for nine months with the purpose of comparing, compiling, checking and completing the oral traditions that had been passed down. The sad ending of the council led to 60,000 monks being excommunicated from the Sangha because they would not adhere to the challenge of Theravada orthodoxy insisted upon by Moggaliputtatissa.

The Spread of Theravada Buddhism

It was reported that King Asoka's brother Mahinda, together with fellow missionaries were those who introduced Buddhism to the King of Ceylon (Sri Lanka), Devanampiya Tissa. This resulted in the fact that later (when Buddhism began to decline in India) Sri Lanka was to become the bastion of Buddhist faith. It is reported that Mahinda proposed to King Tissa that he establish a monastery in the ancient capital of Anuradhapura, called the Mahavihara Temple. This became the centre of Theravada learning. Buddhist scholars from all around flocked to this focal point, among them the famous Buddhaghosa (fifth century AD), who wrote his definitive works and commentaries on the *Dharma* there.

During the ensuing period there was gradual decline of the influence of Buddhism in India so that by the seventh century AD, under increasing pressure from Islamic forces, the main headquarters of the Theravada School had moved to Sri Lanka. Eventually there was virtually no influence and very little evidence of Buddhism having been so powerful in India at all except the uncared for remains of broken down ruins, mere echoes of bygone splendour.

It is said that Mahinda and his companions had memorised the whole of the Buddha's teaching! So it was in Sri Lanka (Ceylon), during the first century BC, that the first recorded writing down of the Scriptures was embarked upon. From this small island the gospel of Theravada Buddhism spread to the regions beyond, particularly into Burma (Myanmar), Thailand, Cambodia, Laos and Vietnam.

Legend asserts that as early as the period of the Buddha's own life time, the Mon people, indigenous to Burma, had built a pagoda to enshrine a relic of the Buddha's hair. This was on the site of the now famous Shwe Pagon Pagoda in the centre of Rangoon. However, the effect of expansion of Buddhism had little impact in that country until AD 1044 under the reign of King Anawrahta an enthusiastic follower of the *Dharma*. He took control and brought unity to the whole country. At this time a famous Mon monk, Shin Arahan, who was an authority in Theravada Buddhism, banished a group of Mahayana monks up country and they constructed the city of Pagan, the most famous centre of Buddhist influence and culture. The King ordered 30,000 captives, and dozens of elephants loaded with relics and Scriptures, to go to Pagan. He not only banished the Mahayana monks, and destroyed their own city, but set out on a campaign to suppress *nat* worship, which was devotion by the local people to animistic spirit powers. By the fourteenth century, Buddhism was dominant and a special council was established called *Mahasangha-Raja* ('the Great ruler of the Sangha'). There were, by this time, up to one million ordained monks in Burma alone.

It is not surprising that Theravada Buddhism spilled over the borders of Burma, going Northward to Southwest China, where the Dai people of Yunnan lived. These people, called 'The Older Brother of the Chinese',[6] are the early ancestors of the Shan people of Northern Burma, the Thai, and Lao peoples. In the eleventh century Northern Thailand was conquered by the Burmese King Ananrahta – one of many wars between the two countries.

The effect of this, combined with the strong influence of the Burmese in Thailand from the seventh century in the south, meant that Thailand adopted Theravada Buddhism as its own state religion under King Ramkhamhaeng in AD 1238. Thais were sent to Ceylon during this Sukhotai Dynasty for further training so that they could be formally ordained into the tradition of Theravada. The early influence of Buddhism in Thailand can be seen from the thousands of temples scattered everywhere throughout the countryside, and from ancient ruins all over the country, especially at the former capital, Ayuttaya.

While battles were raging between Thailand and Burma in the north, other kingdoms were seeking to devour portions of Thailand from the east. After continual warring with the enemy, it was in AD 1353 when Thailand finally threw off the forces of Cambodia and captured their capital, Ankhor. It was from this time that Theravada Buddhism took hold there, and we can see from the beautiful ruins of the now famous Ankhor Wat, how deeply entrenched Buddhism became in that country – until 'the killing fields'.

It was only three years after the fall of the capital of Cambodia, that the King of Laos was converted to Theravada Buddhism (AD 1356). He had been influenced by the King of Cambodia (his father in law) who had sent him a golden Buddha image together with an entourage of monks with the Pali Scriptures as well. Using this image as the centre of worship he built a Buddhist temple in the middle of the capital town Luang Prabang. Buddhism was immediately pronounced the state religion. In 1520 when King Photisarath moved the capital to Vientiane, his son established the city as a holy centre of Theravada Buddhism.

The Expansion of Mahayana Buddhism

Around the commencement of the Christian era, another important development occurred – the emergence of

Mahayana Buddhism otherwise known as 'members of the great community' or 'the Greater Vehicle', in contrast to Theravadins, who claimed to follow 'the Teaching of the Elders' and were called 'the Lesser Vehicle'. In contrasting the difference between the two schools Noss observes:

> When the Mahayanists took their name (Mahayana means 'the Greater vehicle'), the conservative older Buddhism unwillingly accepted the name Hinayana ('the Lesser vehicle'). Vehicle (*yana*) here refers to a means of transportation, such as a raft or ferry, or a carriage. If the crossing of the river analogy is used for Buddhist salvation, the Mahayana is the Great Ferry or Raft and Hinayana the Lesser Ferry or Raft. Besides the rather derogatory juxtaposition of Greater and Lesser, which the Theravadins dislike, there is an implication, some-times pointed out, of Big and Little, the Mahayana being the Big Raft transporting whole groups of believers, with a pilot in charge, and the Hinayana the little Raft for one at a time, or individual transportation.[7]

Theravada Buddhism is severe, strict and conservative, with salvation offered for the few who, with relentless effort, seek enlightenment by their own abandonment of everything else in life. With such a daunting prospect, there are many attractive qualities to Mahayana Buddhism, and this is why the less strict system appealed so much to so many. While it is seen by some as 'compromise', the fact is that it accommodates to people's aspirations, and offers a less rigorous way of attaining Nirvana. More than any-thing else it presents the Bodhisattva figures, 'saints' who have themselves attained the state of Nirvana, but because of their self denying sacrificial love, have deliberately with-held going there in order to offer merit/grace/assistance to lesser mortals who could not get there through their own striving or on their own merits. While in Theravada Buddhism, it is only possible for monks to attain to en-lightenment, and thereby be released into Nirvana, in Mahayana Buddhism the gate of salvation is open for all.

Even the Sangha ceased to be an exclusive 'club' just for those who had left all.

In Mahayana Buddhism, it is said that the Buddha 'sent out' or 'expressed' himself through five 'meditation Buddhas' or 'Dhyanibuddhas'. They are Amitabha, 'the one of immeasurable brilliance'; Vairocana, 'the radiant one'; Akshobya, 'the unshakeable'; Rathnasambhava, 'the one born of precious stones'; and Amonghasiddhi, 'the one of unfailing strength'. These beings can become physically incarnate and appear on earth as the Buddha himself did. They can be called upon for help in times of trouble and are recorded to have come to the rescue of many. Their task is to lead people across the sea of suffering to the place of peace – Nirvana. While this place (*Nirvana*), has the same name as for Theravadins, it is described in a completely different way. Theravadins generally describe Nirvana in terms of what it is not. Mahayana describes a place or state which could be described as Paradise.

The best known description is in the story of Amitabha. As a monk he took an oath that he would become a Buddha if as a result of this a paradise could be formed in which all who prayed to him in the lifetime could live happily after death. The resulting land of Sukhavati or 'paradise of the West' is a place where all hindrances to full salvation are removed, so that the way to Nirvana is clear. This preliminary stage to Nirvana has increasingly become an end in itself where the blessed live in ecstasy after their death.[8]

From this one can see why the expression of Mahayana Buddhism would appeal to the masses. There is less discipline, less devotion, less direction, less demand, less despondency and despair. Even if Nirvana cannot be gained, why not opt for this paradise (elsewhere called 'Pure Land'), which sounds so wonderful, and why not be helped to get there into the bargain, rather than trying to do it all on your own? It was this form of Buddhism that spread so quickly into Tibet, China, Mongolia, Bhutan,

Sikkim and with increasing variations to Japan.

From the following outline, one can clearly see the difference between these two vehicles within Buddhism.

Theravada	Mahayana
Man as an individual	Man as involved with others
Man on his own in the universe (emancipation by self effort)	Man not alone (salvation by grace)
Key virtue: wisdom	Key virtue: *karuna* compassion
Religion: a full-time job (primarily for monks)	Religion: relevant to life in world (for lay people as well)
Ideal: the Arhat	Ideal: the Bodhisattva
Buddha: a saint	Buddha: a saviour
Eschews ritual	Includes ritual
Confines prayer to meditation	Includes petitionary prayer
Conservative	Liberal[9]

'Conservative' relates to the 'restrictiveness' or 'tight discipline' of one school, while 'liberal' relates to the comparative 'laxity' or perceived freedom one may have in the other school.

Apart from the two major divisions within Buddhism, there are a variety of lesser known, but important schools that we will consider briefly. First there is 'Vajrayana' Buddhism a version of Mahayana, which in the middle of the first century AD spread to Nepal, Tibet, China, Mongolia, Korea and Japan.

'Lamaism', became the dominant school in Tibet, and 'Zen' one of the more well-known schools in Japan. There were some other schools in Japan such as The 'Tendai' sect, the 'Shingon' sect, the 'Amida' sect, the 'Nichiren' (circa 13) and its closely related ally, the 'Soka Gakkai' sect, introduced in 1899. This last group has experienced a phenomenal revival since the last world war, with as many as twenty million adherents today.

Vajrayana Buddhism

This form of Buddhism has its own expression in each of the countries mentioned above, but there are characteristics common to them all. There is a strong interest in the mystical, the magical and the occult in this school.[10] Much emphasis is laid on particular techniques which are intended to draw the adherent into 'beyond this world' transempirical experiences. Many of the practices in what is now more clearly known as Tibetan Buddhism emerged from the ancient Indian philosophy of Tantrism. These practices will include special movements of the body with particular emphasis on various Yogic postures. There is a strong focus on eroticism (*shaktiism*) expressed through sexual orgies with precise methodologies in order that the participants would be linked with 'the universal feminine' to realise the ultimate unity of all things. Stress is laid on the use of an endless number of 'mantras' – sounds repeated over and over again, that are purported to have inherent power within themselves, particularly the most well known, '*om mani padme hum*'.

Of special importance in Nepal and Tibet is the *mandala*. This is a circular chart/diagram which represents numerous cosmic and spiritual relationships. Single-minded reflection and contemplation on the power that is purported to emanate from the *mandala* will lead the devotee into out-of-the-body experiences of the divine. A famous book that depicts present life, but more graphically after-death experiences, is called *The Tibetan Book of the Dead*, the Introduction of which states 'as a contribution to the science of death and of the existence after death, and of rebirth *The Tibetan Book of the Dead* called in its own language Bardo Thodol is among the sacred books of the world unique.' In fact much of the book is gruesome – it contains vivid descriptions pictorially and verbally of the Judgment. One such paragraph states 'Then the Lord of Death will place round thy neck a rope and drag thee along; he will cut off thy head, extract thy heart, pull out thine intestines, lick up thy brain, drink thy blood, eat thy flesh and gnaw thy bones; but thou wilt be incapable of dying. Although thy body be hacked into pieces, it will revive again. The repeated hacking will cause intense pain and torture.' Comforting words follow – 'In reality thy body is of the nature of voidness; thou needst not be afraid.'[11]

One particular rendition of Vajrayana Buddhism, exclusive to Tibet, is 'Lamaism'. The word derives from 'one who is a high ranking spiritual leader'. Later the word was used to designate any monk. It can be traced back to the seventh century AD (620–649) when the then King of Tibet, Strong-btsn-sgam-po, introduced this particular school. The Scriptures were translated into Tibetan at this time reinforcing and giving credibility and authority to the teaching. The King's two wives, a princess from Nepal (Bhrikuti daughter of King Amshuvrman) and Princess Wen-cheng, daughter of Thai-tsung, the second Emperor of the Thang dynasty in China, were natural envoys of the new teaching as they journeyed back and forth to their own families and countries respectively. At first there was great hostility in Tibet to the new teaching by the local people who were animistic. However, a certain Padmasambhava who was reported to be the father of Lamaism was a great magic teacher of esoteric Buddhism. On arriving in Tibet from North West India, his combined Yogic skills and Shamanistic powers merged with the Tantric sex symbolism from Hinduism. This attracted the local people and found ready acceptance among them, because much of the teaching echoed some of their own animistic beliefs.

Then followed a period of decline because of corruption and nepotism. In the fourteenth century a Reformer named Tsong-khapa transformed the religion until it regained respectability.

It is out of this reformation that the concept of dual leadership emerged, with one reincarnation of the Buddha addressed as the Dalai Lama, 'the One who is as great as the Ocean' and the other, called the Panchen Lama, 'the Jewel of Scholars'.

Technically speaking as far as devotees are concerned, it is incorrect to think of the Dalai Lama as a normal human being. He is regarded more as the incarnation of a god referred to in the *Lotus Sutra* Scripture, called Avalokitesvara, 'the Lord of mercy, who looks down'. Legend has it that when Avalokitesvara saw the torments of hell, he/she shed two tears from which a female deity Tara was born who was a Bodhisattva or female patron/goddess/saviour in Tibetan Buddhism. Images of Avalokitesvara appear as male in Indian representations, but become female in Chinese representations. It is understood that when a Dalai Lama dies, this god Avalokitesvara is reincarnated into a new body of the succeeding Dalai Lama. Also when a reigning Dalai Lama dies, messengers are sent throughout the world to search for the one who will be recognised as the reincarnation of the deceased Lama or the one in whom the spirit of Avalokitesvara now resides. Numerous auspicious signs are sought for and occult tests are finally undergone in order to establish who is the right reincarnation. If messengers return with more than one name of a child who they think is the correct reincarnation there will be a final ritual to determine the mind of the gods. In this ritual, one of the special monks gifted with oratory invokes the spirit powers who possess him and then in semi-conscious state he involuntarily declares an oracle on behalf of the spirits, determining who is the chosen one.

Similar forms of Mahayana Buddhism spread across South East Asia.

Zen Buddhism

The origins of Zen are lost in the dim distant past. Legend infers that Zen's teaching came direct from Bodhidharma, a mendicant monk living in India 600 years BC. Bodhidharma is said to have shared his beliefs with a Chinese Emperor that truth is transmitted from mind to mind, by-passing the normal use of language. The theme of Zen reemerges much later when the Mahayana school of Buddhism entered China in the first century AD. It was not well received, especially by those who followed the more down to earth plain teaching of Confucianism. About AD 526, the twenty-eighth leader of an Indian sect called Bodhidharma went to China and founded the Ch'an school. One of the most well-known characteristics of this school has been its art depictions of the 'Ten Ox herding Pictures'. While a Westerner may look at the pictures and appreciate their artistic beauty, there is much more to them than appears on the surface. Each picture is a visual aid to depict the various stages of searching for and then finding *satori*, the experience of salvation.[12]

This movement grew apart from its Mahayana roots and became popular to local people in China. It became even more popular to the people of Japan when it was introduced there in the twelfth century. There it became known as 'Zen' (a corruption of the word Ch'an). Its distinctive feature is that there are no particular doctrines that one is obliged to believe. The main emphasis is that one must practise meditation according to various strict rules. This appeal to discipline and strictness was most attractive to the Japanese Samurai warriors of the middle ages and it won a large following during that time.

While everything about Zen appears rather vague, there is a goal-enlightenment (*satori*). This is attained through prolonged, concentrated meditation, in which the devotee assumes the 'lotus position' – sitting cross legged with the base of each foot upwards resting on opposite thighs. Although the process leading to *satori* takes time, the distinctive idea of the main school of Zen is 'the doctrine of abruptness' – that the final experience is immediate and abrupt. The times of meditation, called *zazzen*, are intense and sometimes can last for up to a week, with the goal of reaching enlightenment.

In this daily Zen chanting the sutra known as the Prajna Paramita is always included. The actual sitting itself it preceded by prescribed use of bells, wooden clappers and the exchange of formal bows. Practitioners sit facing a wall or the centre of the zendo, depending on the tradition of the specific sect to which the group belongs, or the preference of the presiding Zen roshi. The position of the hands is strictly specified; they are held in the front of the abdomen, the back of the left in the palm of the right, the thumbs lightly touching. The eyes are not closed, although the gaze is directed downward and is fixed a little in advance of the sitter. Zazen is terminated by the sound of wooden clappers, the ringing of a bell three times and the chanting of the Four Great Vows.[13]

There is a strange paradox and appeal about Zen. The main problem is that it appears to be quite un-reasonable and illogical to the rational mind and yet at the same time it attracts logical thinkers. There have been a plethora of books, written for the Western palate, that have made Zen popular; among them are *Zen and the Art of Motorcycle Maintenance*, *The Zen of Seeing*, and *Zen and Creative Management*.

One important exercise is to meditate on riddles or *koans*. There are nearly two thousand of these and students are obliged to 'experience' the answers, rather than understand them.

These riddles appear to be sense-less, they have no logical meaning or answer, but are intended to transform and raise a person's awareness or thought patterns so as to assist him to gain satori. Here are some examples of typical koans.

'If you meet someone in the street who has reached the truth you may neither walk past him in silence, nor speaking. How then should you meet him?' Or 'When you clap both your hands together a sound results. Now listen to the sound of one hand clapping.' 'A cow passes a window, its head, horns and the four legs all pass by. Why did not the tail pass by?' 'What was the appearance of your face before your ancestors were born?' 'A long time ago a man kept a goose in a bottle. It grew larger and larger until it could not get out of the bottle anymore. He did not want to break the bottle, nor did he wish to hurt the goose; how would you get it out? The Master called out, "O Officer!" "Yes" was the response, "there it is out"!'[14]

No matter how absurd koans appear to be, they are the only way to enlightenment, so one has to submit to the Zen masters who guide and control devotees until they reach a stage of 'intuitive non-rational enlightenment'.

There are differing schools (*Rinzai* and *Soto*) within Zen which clash over views as to whether *satori* is a sudden experience, or a gradual process. We can see that Zen is frustrating because it challenges intellectualism and the supremacy of logic. For this reason it both attracts and intrigues people in the West, but very few are serious enough to devote themselves to its thought processes or practices, with one or two notable exceptions, among them the well known Christian monk Thomas Merton, whose book *On Zen* is renowned. Houston Smith gives us a glimpse of Zen from a Western perspective:

> Entering the Zen outlook is like stepping through Alice's looking glass. One finds oneself in a topsy-turvy wonderland in which everything seems quite mad – charmingly mad for the most part but mad all the same. It is a world of bewildering dialogues, obscure conundrums, stunning paradoxes, flagrant contradictions, and abrupt *non sequiturs*, all carried off in the most urbane, cheerful and innocent style.[15]

One of the most famous Japanese proponents of Zen is Dr Suzuki, spoken of by Christmas Humphries as 'probably the greatest living authority on Buddhist philosophy and certainly the greatest on Zen Buddhism'. He has written eighteen books on Zen in Japanese and his works in English number more than a dozen. He is described by Humphries in the introduction to his book *Essays in Zen*

Buddhism: as one who 'when he speaks of the higher stages of consciousness he speaks as a man who dwells therein, and the impression he makes on those who enter the fringes of his mind is that of a man who seeks for the intellectual symbols wherewith to describe a state of awareness which lies indeed beyond the intellect'.[16]

It would be difficult to summarise in a few lines a book of 350 pages – but the contents page may signify its main thrust. It is separated into two parts. Part one is entitled 'The Koan Exercise (as a means for realising satori or attaining enlightenment)'. This section deals with the true nature of Zen. Part two, 'The Koan Exercise and the Nembutsu' is 'apologetic' in that it defends the true nature of Zen in contrast with 'Nembutsu' – the word meaning 'to think of the Buddha'. This 'Nembutsu' (sometimes known as Pure Land Buddhism) is essentially different from Zen thinking, but has permeated the Zen schools. Suzuki exposes the true nature of what Nembutsu means, when he pictures it as more or less deifying and personalising the Buddha. He reveals the heart of Nembutsu in quoting one of their masters: 'he who intensely longs for the Buddha and thinks of him, will most assuredly come into his presence.' Suzuki states 'those who practise Zen are so exclusively devoted to Zen thinking that they are thus exerting themselves to the attainment of quietude and nothing else; as to invoking the name of the Buddha in order to be born in the Land of Purity and worshipping him and reciting the sutras in the morning and evening they practise nothing of the sort.'[17]

Since Dr Suzuki himself tries to define the nature of satori – by comparing it with Christian experience, it would only be appropriate to use his own comparisons. He states

> Zen experience is that it has no personal note in it as is observable in Christian mystic experiences . . . there is no reference whatever in Buddhist satori to such personal feelings . . . such terms; flame of love, a wonderful love shed in the heart, embrace, spiritual matrimony,

Father, God, the Son of God, God's child, etc. We may say that all these terms have nothing to do with the experience itself. At any rate, alike in China, India and Japan satori has remained thoroughly impersonal or rather highly intellectual. Not only satori itself is such a prosaic and non-glorious event, but the occasion that inspires it also seems to be unromantic, and altogether lacking in super-sensuality. Satori is experienced in connection with any ordinary occurrence in one's daily life; it does not appear to be an extraordinary phenomenon.[18]

There are a number of smaller sects or schools of Buddhism, some of which have contextualised their message and outward forms to fit into Japanese culture. Among them are the Tendai sect, the Shingon sect, the Amida sect and the Shin sect.

The most significant, however, is the Nichiren Shoshu sect, established by a monk named Nichiren in the thirteenth century. Nichiren was born in AD 1222, the son of an ordinary fisherman. This was a time of serious strife and civil war in Japan. Having studied the various forms of Buddhism for himself, Nichiren decided to bring the people back under the authority of the *Lotus Sutra*. He firmly believed that this was the interpretation of the original words of the Buddha and through obedience to it, salvation would come to the masses of people. He enthusiastically went about preaching his findings but his preaching style was so polemical that the authorities were threatened, and finally they threw him into prison. By 1282 when he died, he had attracted a great following.

The main doctrine emphasised is the universality of both the Buddha and humanity so that in the final analysis all will be merged into one common Buddhahood. An extended lay person's development of this was what has now become the most popular of all the sects in Japan, the *Soka Gakkai*, 'The Value Creating Society Sect'. This was introduced into Japan in about 1899 when freedom of religion became constitutional. It stresses lay involvement, together with the importance of duty, loyalty and morality.

Following World War Two when the Emperor declared he was no longer a god:

> The Japanese Government attempted to unify all of Japan under Shinto Buddhism, only Nichiren Shosu refused to obey ... In 1940 there were only 21 members all of whom were arrested. Nineteen of those members converted to Shintoism and finally the only remaining member was Jose Toda who was released from prison in 1945. Under Toda's leadership the movement began growing and elected Toda the second president of Soka Gakkai. In 1960 Daisaku Ikeda was inaugurated president over 1.3 million members.[19]

Under the now renowned Daisaku Ikeda, the movement has mushroomed and become a powerful economic and political force in the land. It is said that there are now more than twenty million adherents. This shows that there must have been a tremendous void or vacuum in the Japanese heart. The *Soka Gakkai* emphasis that sought to combine a re-establishing of some form of religious duty combined with a sense of national pride, cultural identity and physical and emotional well-being, meant that masses of Japanese people embraced this 'contented society'.[20]

The central place of worship for adherents to Nichiren Shosu/Soka Gakkai is a shrine at the foot of Mount Fuji where there is a black wooden box called the *gohonson*. This box contains the names of various important personages recorded in the *Lotus Sutra*. There are purported to be certain cosmic powers within the box that condition and determine events that happen in the life of the believer. The act of worship consists of kneeling before the wooden box and reciting certain passages from the *Lotus Sutra*. A rosary is used as an aid to help the worshipper remember various verses. At the same time the worshipper chants a mantra '*nam-myoho-renegekyo*'.

An important emphasis of this school is its missionary zeal. Members actively proselytise using a method called *shakubuku*, their goal is to bring the whole world under the influence of their belief system. 'Soka Gakkai regards itself as not only the one true Buddhist religion, but the one true religion on earth. Its principal aims are the propagation of its gospel throughout the world by forced conversion if necessary and the denunciation and destruction of all other faiths as 'false' religions. Soka Gakkai is unmistakably a church militant in Japan geared for a determined march abroad.'[21] The following quotation summarises the nature of Buddhism in Japan:

Buddhism is linked to Japanese culture at many points: through the traditional way of the Samurai, generally known as bushido, through the austere 'no' drama with its many themes, through the tea ceremony which is intended to communicate simplicity and naturalness, through calligraphy and painting and so on. The most lively aspects of Japanese Buddhism however remains the popular faith directed towards the various Buddhas, Bodhisattvas and saints of the Mahayana Buddhist tradition.[22]

1. Edward Thomas, *The Life of Buddha as Legend and History* (Routledge & Kegan Paul, 1975), p. 100 quoting from Buddhist Scripture.
2. Ann Bancroft, *Religions of the East* (Heinemann, 1974), p. 81.
3. Christmas Humphries, *Buddhism* (Penguin Books, 1951), pp. 40f.
4. *Mahavaga* 1: 490.
5. Edward Rice, *Eastern Definitions* (Doubleday, 1980), p. 238.
6. William C. Dodds, *The Dai Race – Older Brother of the Chinese* (Torch Press, 1923).
7. J. B. Noss, *Man's Religion* (Macmillan, fifth edition 1974), p. 142.
8. *A Lion Handbook: The World's Religions* (Lion Publishing, 1982), p. 239.
9. Houston Smith, *The Religions of Man* (Harper & Row, 1958), p. 138.

10. See W. Y. Evans-Wentz, *The Tibetan Book of the Dead* (Oxford University Press, third edition, 1963) for more explicit descriptions and explanations.

11. See *The Tibetan Book of the Dead*, p. 166 and also p. 137, The Great Mandala – of wrathful deities.

12. For a detailed explanation of the meaning of the pictures see D. T. Suzuki, *Manual of Zen Buddhism* (Grove Press, 1960), p. 128.

13. Nancy Wilson Ross, *Buddhism: A Way of Thought* (Alfred Knopf Inc., 1980), p. 143.

14. Josh McDowell and Don Stewart, *Understanding Non-Christian Religions* (Here's Life Publishing, 1983), p. 69.

15. Houston Smith, *The Religions of Man*, p. 140.

16. See D. T. Suzuki, *Essays in Zen Buddhism*, second series (Rider & Co., 1970), p. 11.

17. Ibid., p. 11.

18. Ibid., p. 11.

19. Walter Martin (ed.), *The New Cults* (World Vision House Inc., 1980), p. 32.

20. There are at least twenty million adherents of the Soka Gakkai school of Buddhism in Japan today.

21. *Look*, 10 September 1963, p. 16.

22. *A Lion Handbook: The World's Religions*, Part Four: 'Living Religions of the East', p. 266.

3

Sacred Texts and Serious Teachings

Information concerning the teachings of Buddhism comes in two forms, oral and written. It is evident that the oral tradition (the *Sanghas*) was passed down from generation to generation through many centuries before any Scriptures were actually written. Later, a number of official councils were formed to determine the content of the Scriptures.

Buddhist Scriptures were originally written in two languages, Pali and Sanskrit. Sanskrit came to India from Iran nearly two thousand years BC, and was used in the areas of Northern India. In most Western literature there is a notable difference in various spellings of names and places. This is because some writers are using Pali as their source, while others use Sanskrit. The following list (adapted from Pye[1]) illustrates the problem of such discrepancies with various spellings:

Pali	Sanskrit	Meaning and Use
Gotama	Gautama	A clan name, designating persons from common ancestor
Sakyamuni	Shakyamuni	From the 'Sakya Clan' means 'sage of the Sakyas'
Siddhattha	Siddhartha	Personal name given by his father to mean 'mission accomplished'
Bodhisatta	Bodhisattva	'Enlightened one' most often used in Mahayana school in the plural
Buddha	Bodhi	'The awakened one'
Tathagata		'having gone' – a synonym for

		Buddha who has been 'freed'
Arahants	Arahats	'perfected ones'

Theravada Buddhism used the Pali language to write Scripture which is called the Pali Canon. This language is purported to have been a dialect similar to that which Buddha/Gotama would have spoken (Old Maghadhi), and became the popular religious 'high language'. It was carried to Ceylon (Sri Lanka) and became the canonical language used for Theravada Scriptures which monks use consistently for studying and chanting. This would be parallel to English people having to study and chant the New Testament Scripture in its original Greek language.

Most of the contents of the Pali Canon are now the common property of all Buddhist schools. There is an overall harmony, consistency and cohesion about the Pali Canon which suggests a common source, originating with a small number of people who may have had an agreed agenda for format and content. Although there are differences in the other numerous canons, these may have happened because when oral tradition is written down it can be variously expressed, with differing emphasis according to the perception or prejudice of the scribe. The earliest recorded Scriptures written in the Pali language are said to have been written in Sri Lanka about 80 BC, nearly six hundred years after the Buddha was on earth.

Thomas says this about Theravada Scripture:

The Chronicles tell us that in the time of King Vatrtagamani Abhaya (29–17 BC), the monks of Ceylon, seeing the decay of beings, assembled and caused the three Pitakas with their commentary, which they had before handed down orally, to be written in books. This official recording in writing would not exclude the possibility of much of the Canon having already been written, but what is quite certain is that originally and for a long period the Scriptures were preserved only by memory.[2]

The Pali Canon is known as the *Tripitaka*, otherwise interpreted as 'The Three Baskets' because the original documents were written on palm leaf and were kept in three baskets. Each basket contained different elements of teaching. The first (the *Vinayapitaka*) is 'The Basket of (Monastic) Discipline'. This lists and explains all the laws and regulations for those ordained into the monastic Order, including the 227 requirements for each monk. The Second Basket (the *Sutra-pitaka*), is entitled 'The Basket of Discourses' containing much of the Buddha's teachings. The third basket (the *Abhidhamma-pitaka*) which supplements the second is called 'The Basket of Further Teachings' and centres on a systematic analysis of the Buddha's teaching as it applies to human experience. When translated, the second basket comprises forty-two quite large volumes. Within these volumes, there are listed numerous discourses, recitations, stories of the departed, instructions for nuns, chronicles of the lives and existences of twenty-four previous Buddhas, and analyses of various points of doctrine.[3] One of the most popular sections of this basket, translated more than any other, is the *dhammapada* or *dhamma* (not to be confused with *The Dharma*, the word used for all the teachings of the Buddha collectively). The *dhammapada* is a collection of 423 verses almost wholly giving ethical instructions. Another section, probably *the* most popular, which could be likened to Western fairy tales, has already been referred to and is called the *Jataka*. This is a collection of 547 'apocryphal' 'birth stories' (six volumes) recording the previous lives and adventures of the Buddha. Although most surmise that this is a very late addition to the canon, it is continually referred to in sermons because of its supernatural, sensational and dramatic elements.

The followers of the Theravada school insist that their Scriptures are the pure and unadulterated form of the Buddha's teaching. However, in view of the fact that they were penned 500 years after the death of the Buddha, from a Western point of view there will always be some question concerning the accuracy of the records. This is because of a Western dependence on written tradition rather than oral. Nevertheless, Schumann states: 'to assume that pre-canonical Buddhism was essentially different from Pali Buddhism, is sheer speculation.'[4]

Central Themes from the Three Baskets in the Pali Canon

The overarching philosophical basis for the Buddha's teaching was triggered by the traumatic shock he experienced when he 'went beyond the wall' of the palace, as a young man and was confronted with the reality of suffering. The whole system and structure of Buddhism is conditioned and limited by this one fundamental question – why suffering? (For a detailed description of the main tenets of Buddhism, see Chapter 4.)

In the Buddha's first message to his five followers he stated:

> This monks, is the Noble Truth of Suffering (dukkha). Birth is suffering, old age is suffering, illness is suffering, death is suffering; grief, lamentation, pain, affliction and despair are suffering; to be united with what is unloved, to be separated from what is loved is suffering; not to obtain what is longed for is suffering; in short the Five Groups of Grasping are suffering.[5]

Suffering is classified into three basic categories, and 'the five groups of grasping'. The three 'cause' categories are:

1. Suffering resulting from pain.
2. Suffering resulting from the nature of change or impermanence.
3. Suffering resulting from the fact of actually existing as an individual.

Actual existence as an individual human being, (having human nature or 'self-hood'), is defined in terms of 'the five groups of grasping' enumerated by the Buddha. These 'groups' (combinations or aggregates) are called *skandhas*.

When they all come together at one time, they are what can be defined as the nature of 'human-being'. They are:

1. The group of grasping – 'body' (*rupa*) having a human body, comprising earth, water, fire and wind.
2. The group of grasping – 'sensation' (*vedana*): the normal responses of the five senses – seeing, hearing, tasting, touching and smelling.
3. The group of grasping – 'perception' (*sannya*): perceptive reaction of one's feelings to whatever has been the cause of something.
4. The group of grasping – 'mental phenomena' (*samkhara*): reaction of the will.
5. The group of grasping – 'consciousness' (*vinnana*): reaction of the intellect.

Two words are used to define 'humanness', one *ruba* for the physical body, the other *nama* for those other parts which constitute our 'human-being', that are not physical.

Ruba (literally meaning 'shape' or 'form') relates to a human being's physical stature, comprising its various *skandhas* – sometimes in Buddhist literature defined in terms of the four elements, earth, water, fire and air.

Nama covers the other four groups of grasping and relates to the non-physical components of self-hood. They are:

1. 'Sensations': these are empirical responses relating to how one gains perception through the use of one's senses.
2. 'Mental phenomena': the faculty that enables one to understand the nature of the external world.
3. 'Internal impressions': relates to intentions, ideals, moods, concepts, intuitions etc.
4. 'Consciousness': relates to an awareness or understanding of the impermanence of existence or self-hood. It can also mean cognisance that our momentary existence can only happen through the embodiment of 'universal energies' of good and bad forces.

Personal existence therefore, predicates the merging of the five *skandhas* of grasping at any one time. This state of 'being' or coming into existence is regarded as synonymous with 'suffering'. One cannot '*be*' without suffering; they are the same. This then leads to the concept of *annica* – transience, or impermanence. The *skandhas* only come together for however long a lifetime is. And however long a lifetime is, is *dukkha* – suffering.

Out of these statements various philosophical propositions have been made. Some say that because human beings are made up of the tangible elements of earth, water, fire and air, then a person is simply the sum of 'matter' – what else is there in the universe? Human beings cannot therefore possess a 'self' or 'soul' (*anatta*).

The Buddha did seem to affirm this principle of 'non-self-hood', which together with the notion of non-transference of 'souls' related to the teaching of reincarnation, is a major departure from Hinduism.

This new *skandha* concept means that because a human being is constituted solely as a result of a combination of various elements coming together at any one time, it is therefore impossible for anything to pass from one appearance (reincarnation) of non-selfhood to another, apart from what is termed *karma*. This can be defined as an immutable law of cause and effect, where the 'weight' of good or bad merit a person possesses in the present will have been transferred from a previous existence. As indicated, this teaching is a radical departure from the Hindu concept of the 'transmigration of souls', which means the *continuity of personhood* between one reincarnation and another. If the concept is that only 'merit' is transferred, rather than personality or personhood, then it raises the difficulty of defining the true nature of reincarnation.

It is clear from the emphasis of Theravada Buddhism in the Pali Canon, that rebirth does occur, but without the transmigration of the previous person/animal (being), 'personality' or soul. Such 'impact' of one 'non-self' in a past life, upon another 'non-self' in the present, could be compared to the impact of billiard balls upon each other. While nothing is transferred upon impact between one ball and the other, the second ball is set in motion (karmic law), by the first and the second ball can in turn change the course and direction of a third with no transference of the nature of one ball upon another. So with rebirth, each 'condition' or rebirth, 'conditions' subsequent rebirths, but there is no silk thread of continuity, which would link the individual pearls of 'personhood' on the string of subsequent existences. This is called 'conditioned origination' or 'the nexus of conditioned origination'. The Pali name is *paticcasamuppada*.

The effect of the coming together of these 'five groups of grasping' as one particular person, can only normally be traced back to three pre-existences of selfhood. In other words the impact or power of the billiard balls can only be traced back for three pre-existences – after that it (the karmic force) appears to peter out. This of course will not be the case when one is fully enlightened, for attainment to such a state means that one can trace back one's reincarnations almost infinitely as the Buddha did.

In simple terms all of this means that anything material that emerges or exists (human beings), must come into being because of certain conditions (the five *skandhas* coming together), and logically will cease to exist when those conditions are removed. As everything has a cause, so everything must have an effect – but one must not perceive the 'cause' in terms of a beginning in a linear way, but in terms of 'no-beginning' in a cyclical way. This is why the 'wheel' motif is so important in Buddhism. The *origin* of causation then has no *origin* or beginning. Nobody can determine where a wheel begins or where it ends. So it is with the wheel of suffering. Schumann clarifies this for us:

Just as arranged sounds make up a melody, so do conditional ephemeral phenomena constitute the chain of existences. The Nexus of Conditioned Origination = empirical person suffering – this is the formula which underlies the Buddhist conception of man.[6]

Certain important 'trigger words' in the Pali Canon help to define how the nexus of conditioned origination operates – some of the words are: Ignorance: (*Avija*): 'ignorance' or 'having no knowledge of' – implies a lack of knowledge of the way of escape from suffering through the Four Noble Truths. Some well-known teachers have reinterpreted the word *avija* applying it to a Creator (if there was one), for whoever or whatever created this mess of a world must be named *avija* (ignorant) simply because nobody with common sense would have allowed such a world to exist.

Volition *Samskhara* (*Cetana*): relates to purposefulness, or intention expressed in thought and action. It is specifically focused upon purposefulness in terms of determination to follow the middle way.

Non-self (*annata*): 'Non-self-hood' – the belief that there can be found no permanent ego within human personality. Sometimes this is interpreted as emptiness of self, in the sense of annihilation of personal ego, or self-centredness.

Self-hood (*atman*): the opposite of non-self, permanent self-hood. This idea derives from Hinduism where it was thought that behind everything there is a common 'Brahmin' force which unifies everything into itself. This is opposite to the *skandha* belief of all things being in a state of momentary flux.

Paradoxically monks address themselves using '*atman*', as a personal pronoun. This permanent selfhood concept is regarded as a great fallacy or illusion, by Theravada Buddhists. They only see 'persons', as momentary collections of the five *skandhas* already mentioned. Personhood at this split second is not the same as it was a second ago and will not be the same in one second's time. It can be likened to standing on a bridge and looking at the fast flowing water under the bridge. The water at any second of passing can be called water, but its essential elements are changed at every moment. So while what is flowing under the bridge at one second can truly appear to be the same, it can also be truly said that it is not after all, the same water that flowed a split second later – our 'humanbeingness' is therefore simply 'water under the bridge'.

The Mahayana Scriptures

The Mahayana Scriptures, often called *Sutras*, are thought to have been composed by anonymous authors between the first century BC and the sixth century AD. The thirty-eight books were written in Sanskrit which was the most popular and prestigious *lingua franca* of the time. In mentioning these Scriptures, Harvey indicates: 'While many are attributed to Buddha, their form and content clearly show that they were later re-statements and extensions of the Buddha's message.'[7]

There are two main foci within the *Sutras*. The first centres on devotion directed toward a more than human Buddha, it extends to virtual adoration of the concept, with belief in the anticipated coming of a future Buddha 'Metteya' – literally a 'prince of peace'. The second deals with the more philosophical elements of Buddhism, mainly the concept of spiritual wisdom and the idea of oneness with the 'Absolute' – the essence of everything that exists. This emphasis has familiar 'echoes' from its source, Hinduism.

Because of the differing focus and emphasis of the devotees, their pathways diverged, while both claimed ultimate authority. From the Sanskrit Scriptures, especially the *Lotus Sutra*, there emerged a supernaturalistic world view and a Buddha hardly recognisable as the same person in the Pali Canon. This 'superman' is depicted in the biography *Mahavitsu* as a wonder worker with limitless powers, able to control natural and demonic spiritual forces. A later document *Lalitavistara* presents the life of the Buddha as an enactment or paradigm of life. The *Saddharmapundarikasutra* 'Lotus of the Good Law' (*Lotus Sutra*) presents the essence of Mahayana teaching,

that the Buddha is a universal Saviour, the bestower of
salvation – not only through his teaching, but actually in
himself.

Some *Sutra* quotations reflect this deification of the
Buddha who is purported to have claimed concerning
himself:

> Inconceivable thousands of millions of world-ages
> whose duration can never be fathomed it is, since I first
> obtained enlightenment; (since then) I continually
> expound the teaching.
>
> (1) I seize (with the teaching) numerous Bodhisattvas
> and transpose them into Buddha-knowledge. During
> many millions of world-ages I make many million
> myriads of beings mature (to enlightenment).
>
> (2) I delude (beings into seeing) the sphere of Nirvana.
> As a means to (moral) discipline I tell beings (about it).
> I am, however, not extinct; I am here (in the world) and
> reveal the teaching.
>
> (3) When (i.e. men) regard me as perfectly extinct
> (*parinirvtra*) they offer manifold worship to the relics.
> They do not see me and therefore develop desire (for
> me). By that their minds become candid.
>
> (5) When beings are candid, gentle, forbearing and
> free from greed, then I hold a congregation of disciples
> and reveal myself to them on the Vulture Peak.
>
> (6) And then I speak thus to them: 'Monks, I am not
> extinct here (in this world) (My apparent extinction) was
> a clever trick of mine (to encourage beings). Again and
> again I am born in the world of living beings.

Schumann interprets this:

> According to this, the earthly life of the Buddha
> Gautama, and his Nirvana are illusions which the time-
> less and transcendent Buddha projected on to the world
> in order to lead mankind to knowledge and virtuous
> conduct.[8]

'Pure' Sanskrit language, and 'Hybrid Sanskrit' which was a combination of Sanskrit with other local dialects, was widespread throughout India, but particularly in the North – and the Northern school of Buddhism (Mahayana) wrote their Scriptures in this language. Gard helps put together this jigsaw of the linguistic origins and geographic development of the Buddhist Scriptures:

> Therefore neither scripture was translated from the other. The Pali scriptures were translated in Sinhalese, Burmese, Cambodian, Laotian, Mon, Thai and Roman letters (the Pali Text Society edition). The Buddhist Hybrid Sanskrit scriptures were developed in various scripts; Brahma, Kharosthi, Gupta, Devangari, Sidhamatrka, and Kava (Old Javanese). Further Translations of Buddhism Hybrid Sanskrit were made into Khotanese, Sogidian and Turkish in Central Asia. From these, as well as from Buddhist Hybrid Sanskrit and some Pali and Sanskrit, other scripts such as Chinese, Korean, Japanese, and Vietnamese were developed and from the Buddhist Hybrid Sanskrit and some Central Asian and Chinese languages, translations were made into Tibetan and Mongolian.[9]

Westerners have had to depend largely on the Chinese and Tibetan Buddhist canons for their understanding of Mahayana Buddhism because more has been translated into English from these languages than from the original Sanskrit. Most of the Pali Canon of Theravada Buddhism has already been translated into English by the Pali Text Society.

In contrast to the comparatively small Pali Canon of Scripture 'owned' or recognised by those who follow the Theravada school as their authority for understanding the *Dharma*, the Mahayana school boasts a multiplication of over 5,000 volumes! Almost all the text of the Pali Canon is incorporated into these Sanskrit Scriptures, but there appear to be no clear limits to the extent of the Mahayana Canon of Scripture. It is impossible for any single believer to read, interpret or understand such a vast library of books, which in themselves often have paradoxical or, as some would see, contradictory statements.

The Tibetan Canon

The specific contribution of texts of the Tibetan tradition are called *Tantras* which do not supersede the Mahayana Scriptures, but add to them. They are called *Mantrayana* (the Vehicle of Mantra). The origins of the Tantras emerge from the Tantric tradition of Hinduism. This was based on the relationship (sometimes overtly sexual) between the deity Shiva and his consort Shakti. The claim of Tantrism is that through its methodologies and techniques, it can accelerate the devotees' progress to Buddhahood. Tibetan Buddhism is very eclectic, drawing together elements from Mahayana, Tantric, and parts of Tibet's traditional animistic Bon religion.

History records two main advances of Buddhism into Tibet. The first, in about 640 BC, came through King Songtse Gampo whose marital affairs appeared to be diplomatic, political and convenient. He was first married to the Chinese Emperor T'aitsung's daughter and then to Bhrikuti a daughter of the King of Nepal. Both wives were ardent Buddhists and introduced Buddhism through invitations to Buddhist monks from these countries. It is reported that King Songtse even translated some texts from the Buddhist Scriptures himself.

During the eleventh to twelfth centuries, history records that there was much going to and fro between Tibet and India. Many curious Tibetans began visiting Buddhist monasteries in Northern India and with great interest took back with them many Buddhist Scriptures. Following this, many Tibetans began to receive training as monks, studying in India, and then ostensibly becoming missionaries to their own people. By 1042, through the influence of the famous Indian Buddhist scholar Atisa who took the *Dharma* with him, Buddhism became established as the dominant religion. Through this new movement major works of translation began:

> Including the Bka'gyur ('translation of the Buddha Word') and Bstang'gyur ('The translations of the Teachings') collections. The Bka'gyur contains six sections: (1) Tantra (2) Prajnaparamita (3) Ratnakuta a collection of small Mahayana texts, (4) Avatamsaka (5) Sutra (mostly Mahayana sutras, but some Hinayana texts are included), and (6) Vinaya. The Bstan'gyur contains 224 volumes with 3,626 texts, divided into three major groups (1) storras (hymns of praise) in one volume including 64 texts (2) Commentaries on Tantras in 86 volumes including 3,055 texts and (3) Commentaries on sutras in 137 volumes including 567 texts.[10]

One can see that it would take a life time of intense study to be able to comprehend the contents of this massive amount of material. Reference to the renowned text on Tibetan Buddhism, *The Tibetan Book of the Dead,* is made in Chapter 9.

Chinese Versions

Although there were many advances into China by various Buddhist emissaries, they were at times misunderstood because of differences of interpretation between a Taoist world-view and the Buddhist world-view. It was not until the decline and fall of the Han dynasty (AD 220) that various Buddhist texts were translated into Chinese. Much later, in AD 400, a renowned translator Kumarajiva with a team of helpers translated vast numbers of Buddhist texts from Sanskrit into Chinese. The Chinese version 'contains 55 volumes with 2,184 texts, and a supplement of 45 volumes'[11]. Harvey indicates that this was perhaps the greatest translation project the world has ever seen. It is also important to remember it was during this period that

the Chinese (not Gutenberg) invented printing and produced the oldest printed book in the world. This was a
copy of the *Diamond Perfection of Wisdom Sutra* printed
in AD 86.

The *Lotus Sutra* became the most popular of all
translations; it gripped the imagination of the Chinese,
because it presented the Buddha, not as just another
teacher like their own famous teachers Confucius or Lao-
tzu, but as one who had all the supernatural attributes of
God.

Various Schools of Buddhism in China

There have been at least eight schools of Buddhism in
China, the most distinctive of which is the Ch'an (pronounced Zen in Japanese). There are also the Tantric
school, the Theravada school, and most well known and
easy to follow, the simplest Pure Land school.

Ch'an Buddhism
The word 'Ch'an' comes from the Sanskrit and means 'to
meditate'. This school therefore places particular emphasis
on the art of meditation. This form of Chinese Buddhism
could be likened to a Neapolitan 'swirl' or a 'pick and
mix' of religious ideas drawn from ancient India; it was
purported to have been brought to China by an Indian
mendicant monk. Add to the Indian base, a mix of Taoism,
a heavy application of Mahayana thought, some Confucianism, and you have Ch'an. Then introduce some extra
new ingredients hitherto unrelated to Buddhist practice,
such as the martial arts, and the requirement for monks to
engage in physical labour and you have a recipe which
was quite revolutionary. Even more important than this
were some of the doctrinal features. First, that Buddhahood (enlightenment) could be attained instantaneously,
and that *meditation* was more important than *study* of the
Scriptures in order to arrive at this state. All of this was so
new to Buddhist ideology, that it produced a powerful

ripple effect throughout the various monasteries and hierarchies of Buddhism. The concept of *koan* now so popular in Japanese Zen, also originated in Cha'an. A *koan* is the deliberate choice and use of all sorts of weird expressions, phrases or stories, that are totally un-intelligible and meaningless to the normal thinking processes, but 'meaningful' to those who possess under-standing that goes beyond the rational. There is more about this under the subject of Zen (see Chapter 2).

Pure Land Buddhism

This is derived from the Mahayana school, but has its own particular Chinese application. A former Taoist called Hui-yuan discovered some ancient Buddhist Scriptures in Sanskrit called the *Sukhavativyuha Sutra* and from this he ascertained that a Bodhisattva called *Dharmakara* had made certain vows, among which was a promise that whoever looked to him, and depended upon him for his help, would be saved. This Bodhisattva was finally re-incarnated as Buddha *Amitabha* who established a 'Pure Land' which would only be attainable through faith in *Amitabha*. Faith should be expressed in four ways, by continual repetition of his name, by chanting the *Ambitabha Sutra*, by a process of meditation and finally by giving alms and making obeisance to his images.

It is clear from all this that there is a vast amount of literature available within the various schools of Buddhism.

Seven Common Doctrines that Lead to Deliverance

It has already been stated that there are large areas of doctrine in Buddhism that are common to all schools. Schumann has analysed the various schools and strands of Buddhism, with their *different* distinctive features but suggests that there is a strong undercurrent flowing in the same direction which is *common* to all of them; or perhaps one should be more precise by indicating at least seven undercurrents. They are as follows:

1. The Way of Self-discipline

This is obviously the most important common theme. Following the Noble Eightfold Path (common to all) should result in the eradication of craving, sloth, ignorance and lust. It is important to note that while the principles of self-discipline are common to all, there can be very great differences in the practices or methodologies to aid development of self-discipline. Some will tend towards a preoccupation with study, some with meditation, some with seeking mystical experiences, some with following prescribed techniques, some in total isolation, some in community. The most important difference would be that in Theravada, there is perceived to be no help from anyone beyond oneself; one must walk the pathway alone. Whereas in Mahayana (for the most part), there will be the added comfort of knowing that somewhere along the way, waiting in the wings, the Bodhisattvas will be prepared to come on to the stage of one's fleeting existence to bring help to those in need.

2. Meditation

Again this is common to all schools in principle, but in practice there will be multifaceted ways and means of engaging in the process. Many of these numerous methods of meditation are described in Chapter 6.

3. The Value of Wisdom

The expressions *vija* – wisdom and *avija* – ignorance, are extremely common words in the Pali Canon and of equal importance in the *Prajnaparamita* literature of the Mahayana school. In fact the word *Prajnaparamita* simply means 'wisdom literature'.

4. The Bodhisattva Way

There would seem to be very little common ground in this respect, since in Theravada Buddhism there are no Bodhisattvas – but there may be ways to get round this. One of the principal purposes or functions of the Bodhisattva is to 'transfer merit' to another person in need. It has been argued that this concept is alien to the orthodox Theravada school. Nevertheless, a popular belief holds that it *is* possible for even ordinary monks to transfer merit to others, as well as those other beings higher up the scale of power and importance. A well-known popular saying for the ordinary devotee in one Asian language says 'I cling on to the saffron robe (of the monk), in order that I may be taken to heaven.' This indicates a dependency upon and transference of another's merit in order to gain salvation.

5. The Way of Devotion or Faith
This naturally is a common thread throughout all schools. Although again, the form of devotion will be different, the goal is the same – deliverance from suffering.

6. The Cultic Way
This is worship of relics (teeth, hair, footprints or other parts of the Buddha's anatomy), stupas, images, icons, sacred places. The purist idea would be to interpret any outward forms or images as mere aids to remember the Buddha, the *Dharma*, or a particularly famous godly Buddhist priest. However, the vast majority of devotees secretly hope that when they bow down and pray there really is someone listening who is first able to help and second willing to answer their petition.

7. The Way of the Mantras
This is again a common element in all branches of Buddhism. Mantras are vocalisations of sounds or words, that are believed to have magical powers in themselves. They are chanted by devotees individually or as a congregation. Their visual counterpart called '*yantras*' are 'hieroglyphics', which comprise all sorts of 'squiggles' in all sizes and shapes. They may appear to be meaningless to the uninitiated, but to the believer they are as powerful as mantras and can be used for protection in vehicles, as bandages for healing and as protection in war. A common yantra is a straight line starting from the top which

gradually begins to spiral out, so that it is supposed to represent the Buddha sitting in lotus position on the coils of the guardian snake.

1. Michael Pye, *The Buddha* (Duckworth, 1979), p. 2.
2. Edward Thomas, *The Life of Buddha in Legend and History* (Routledge & Kegan Paul, 1975), p. 147.
3. For details of the contents of the three baskets, see Peter Harvey, *An Introduction to Buddhism* (Cambridge University Press, 1990), p. 323.
4. H. W. Schumann, *Buddhism* (Rider & Co., 1973), p. 36.
5. Ibid., p. 38.
6. Ibid., p. 64.
7. Harvey, *Introduction to Buddhism*, p. 4.
8. Schumann, *Buddhism*, pp. 99–100.
9. R. Gard, *Buddhism* (George Braziller, 1962), pp. 44–47, cited in H. S. Shin, *The Thought and Life of Hinayana Buddhism* (OMF Publishing, Bangkok, 1990), p. 58.
10. *Encyclopaedia Britannica* (fifteenth edition, 1992), Vol. 15, p. 275.
11. Ibid., p. 323.

Chalk and Cheese – or Just Two Cheeses? A Comparison of Doctrines

It is recognised universally that the main focus of Buddhism is on the nature of suffering and how to escape from it. It is also generally agreed that the main focus of Christian teaching centres on the nature of sin and how to be forgiven. If this difference is not understood from the beginning, one may be mistaken for thinking that the two systems of belief are seeking to answer the same problem, but this is patently not the case. As has been stated elsewhere, if the diagnosis of a disease is different, then the prescribed medicine for its cure will be different. For this reason it is necessary to consider what 'suffering' really means, and indeed what 'sin' really means, from both a Buddhist and a Christian perspective.

The Nature of Suffering

While accepting much common ground regarding suffering for both Buddhist and Christian, there is nevertheless a fundamental distinction between the First Noble Truth of Buddhism, 'the fact of suffering', which one has to admit, lends itself to a rather pessimistic outlook on life, and the biblical recognition of the same concept that 'human beings are born to trouble as surely as the sparks fly upward'; which at first sight looks almost equally as gloomy. Nevertheless, for the Christian, one does not have to escape from suffering; it can be transformed from something inherently destructive, into something constructive and redemptive. The Buddhist may argue that suffering can also be beneficial since it may accelerate the journey along the path to enlightenment. We will see that both the cause and the effect of being released from either suffering or sin are very different within the two belief systems.

In a nutshell, the fundamental different between Christ and the Buddha on this subject is that Christ's emphasis is on the *importance of moral evil,* and how to deal with it, while central to the Buddha's teaching is the *importance of suffering* and how to escape from it. This does not mean that Christ overlooked the *reality* of suffering. He understood fully the teaching of the Old Testament prophet Isaiah, a contemporary of the Buddha, that he would himself be the fulfilment of prophecies concerning his own identity as 'the *Suffering* Servant'. Understanding of the nature of suffering from a Buddhist point of view could be paralleled with Job's friends, again in the Old Testament, who maintained that Job's suffering must have been caused by his evil deeds, which would inevitably bring a just retribution upon him because of the law of cause and effect. The fact of Job's innocence would be inconceivable as far as his friends were concerned.

In similar vein, there is no answer in Buddhism to the question – why do the *righteous* suffer, while the *wicked* flourish? The Buddha resolved this problem with the doctrine of *karma,* which either attributes bad moral deeds as the cause of suffering, or denies its existence – for according to karma, there can be no *innocent* suffering, since all suffering is punishment justly earned by misdeeds in a previous incarnation. It is true that many people of Jesus's time held the same idea, but Jesus repudiated this predestinational view that exceptional misfortune is predictable evidence of, and punishment for exceptional sin. He pointed out that the eighteen people who died when the tower of Siloam collapsed were no worse sinners than his listeners who had not met such a fate (Luke 13:4). So, it was not the *fact* of suffering that was overlooked by

Jesus, it was the *meaning* of suffering that was interpreted in a completely different way.

Streeter points out:

> The problem of human life as it presented itself to the Buddha's mind, would have seemed to Christ unduly simplified. The Babylonian exile, followed by centuries of oppression by foreign power, had made suffering for the Jew a problem of national experience, as well as of individual, to an extent unparalleled elsewhere in human history. Christ speaks of pain much less than does Buddha, but he knew more about it. And for him there was a graver problem. The history of his people, as interpreted by a long line of prophets, had concentrated attention, again to an extent unique in human history, on the problem of moral evil, both in the individual and in social life. To the Buddha we have seen, the problem of moral evil was incidental to the problem of pain: immoral action tends to increase the will to live, there the overcoming of evil impulses in the soul is a precondition of deliverance from pain. It was impossible for a Jew either to explain suffering by means of Karma, or to think of sin as something incidental. Thus to Christ the problem of evil had been posed on a larger scale than to Buddha: and paradoxically enough, it was a problem made at once more difficult and more hopeful of solution because it had been written 'God saw that it was good'.[1]

The biblical escape mechanisms from this whirlpool of misery and suffering differ logically from the escape mechanisms of Buddhism, because there are different interpretations, both with regard to the nature of ultimate reality, and the cause and effect of moral evil and suffering. At the risk of repetition, one can only prescribe a proper cure according to a correct diagnosis.

Although Buddhism and Christianity do share much common ground in regard to the nature of suffering there are nevertheless some important extensions to the meaning of suffering which are quite unique to Buddhism.

The First Noble Truth: The Fact of Suffering

Suffering, for the Buddhist, includes not only the usual physical, mental or functional dimensions of living, but it goes much further and includes the very fact of 'living', the ontological 'state of being' or actual existence. To have individualised existence, is suffering. 'Self' is *per se*, the expression of desire, and the fact that desire is 'there', is simply because of personal 'being' or existing. Put simply, birth is suffering, decay is suffering, death is suffering, so to exist is to suffer. The fact of existence is characterised by three things: impermanence, non-substance, and suffering.

> So it is that the Buddha said that all things relating to sense and life are on fire – with the fire of that desire which leads on to ever new birth-death experiences: and this is why he elsewhere called the body a 'wound'. The body, or our physical sense capabilities, is a wound because it is a continual source of agitation and distress to man. Hence he can never be at peace in the body. And it is also a wound because it is a breach in man's spiritual impregnability through which pour in the un-spiritual infections of an order of existence driven by craving. Indeed, the total individualised existence of man is a wound. Mind-body individuality is an eternally bleeding, reinfecting painful wound, producing a continual restless disease in man, deeper and more pervasive than any of his specific ills.[2]

The Second Noble Truth: The Origin of Suffering

This 'dis-ease' of humanity from a Buddhist perspective is presented as the Second Noble Truth: the discovery that the three poisons, ignorance, attachment, and hatred are the cause of suffering. But behind these three poisons is the principal cause of suffering which is 'ignorance'. Attaining enlightenment will banish this ignorance, through the realisation that suffering can cease, as follows:

The Third Noble Truth: The Extinction of Suffering

'Suffering ceases when desire ceases.' The 'good news' of Buddhism is this Third Noble Truth. That is, those who really acknowledge the first two truths *can* be released from suffering. This release will finally be reached by following

The Fourth Noble Truth

This comprises the Eightfold Path, otherwise called the 'middle way'. Adherence to the Eightfold Path should lead to release and detachment, which will in turn produce a state where personhood, 'humanbeingness', is dissolved and individual existence evaporates 'like a drop of water into an ocean of nothingness', called Nirvana.

The Eightfold Path, indicated below, is essentially concerned with three areas of human behaviour: morality, spiritual discipline, and insight:

1. Right knowledge or understanding: A recognition and understanding of the Four Noble Truths.
2. Right attitude and desires (right mindedness): Freedom from lust, hatred, selfishness and cruelty.
3. Right speech: Lying, gossiping, and harsh or unkind language, are totally unacceptable. Instead, speech should be wise, truthful, and aimed at reconciliation and peace.
4. Right conduct (right action): This embraces all moral behaviour. In Buddhism morality and intellectual enlightenment are inseparable.
5. Right livelihood: Every aspect of life must be governed by the principle that nothing one does should be harmful to any other creature.
6. Right effort: Every endeavour is made to ensure that evil thoughts and desires be subdued and good thoughts fostered.
7. Right mindfulness or awareness: The conscious act of not submitting to desires and emotions.
8. Right concentration or meditation: This demands a single mindedness of thought so that one is freed

from all distractions, thus leading to tranquillity and finally Nirvana.

Attempting to meet the rigorous standards of this belief system does, for some, result in a feeling of futility, despondency and fatalism. Not only may devotees perceive themselves as having been walking the treadmill of endless existences in the past, seemingly getting nowhere, but ahead of them too there appear to be more existences which karma has inexorably predestined them to follow.

> To a believer in Karma, death is no escape: it is only a preliminary to a new series of rebirths – perhaps in Hell for an aeon, perhaps on earth as an animal, as a woman, as a pariah, or as a man whose life is more crowded with disappointment and disaster than that from which death seemed a refuge. If death is no escape from human misery, but merely a portal to rebirth, something must be found to break the chain of cause and effect which makes that rebirth necessary. This, to the Buddha, can be done by the eradication of 'desire', that is, of the will-to-live, which is the primal cause of birth and continued rebirth: and it can be done in no other way. To this end a man must realise that his individual self belongs, like other phenomenal objects, to the realm of *MAYA*. And he must know the individual self to be illusion, not merely with the pure intellect, but also with that deeper realisation which can be achieved only by a long discipline of negating every personal desire.[3]

It quite often happens that the ordinary Buddhist will almost instinctively resist the call to total detachment from this life because, after all, living down here does have its attractions. Such a person may not realise that possessing an attitude towards life like this, may mean being condemned to the appalling prospect of future eternities dominated by craving and imprisoned by the endless cycle of birth and death. Suffering indeed. A person may try to blame karma for the past, but it is present deeds and attitudes that will determine the future – how awesome and fearful a predicament. Winston King paints the picture of humanity seen from this perspective:

> This then is man according to Buddhism: an eternally individualised, infinitely repetitive projection of the will-to-be into ever new forms, of which his present being is but one. The difference from the Christian view of man is obvious. The Buddhist view sharply qualifies or even undercuts the Christian sense of the 'worth' of the unique human individual that grows out of the latter's historicity and personalism. Or at the very least it places the worth of man in a very different context. And since this so basically colours the Buddhist approach to man's problem and to human life and activity in general, it is most important to grasp its real significance. It may therefore help if the Buddhist view of man is phrased thus *'the fundamental root of man's misery is his existence as a personalised individual'* and for whatever form of Buddhism we survey, this holds true. The *'fall'* of man, according to Buddhism, was his *'fall'* into individualised sentient being.[4]

One may conclude that individual existence as such is essentially *dukkha* suffering. So the quality of *dukkha* pervades the life of the Buddhist as guilt does for the Christian. But unlike the Christian whose past guilt can be dealt with here and now, there is no release from *dukkha* for the Buddhist until existence comes to an end.

So, it is true that while some perceptions of the Buddhist and Christian are similar, it would be wrong to conclude that they are the same. The Christian for example accepts that the world, as originally created, was essentially 'good'. Therefore, because creation was essentially good, human beings can still appreciate the wonder and beauty of creation – they can even become 'attached' to it, without feeling guilty.

D.T. Niles, on the subject of the cause and cure for suffering *and* sin, suggests that there can be salvation from *dukkha* – suffering, but only if we recognise that the primary problem is not *dukkha*, but *doha* – sin. He explains:

> Until and unless this evil is dealt with, both in the world and in us, there is no final solution to the problem of living. For life's basic ill is not Dukkha but Doha – that attitude of rebellion and disloyalty which we have toward God, who is the ground of our being, the final cause of the world and the purpose which gives meaning to life. The cause of Dukkha is my clinging to self; it is this same self-centralism which is also the cause of Doha: the unconscious or conscious assumption that I hold within myself the clue to life's meaning and can of myself discover and obey that clue. Dukkha comes as a result of the self's craving to satisfy itself with the things of this world: it comes as a result of the self's attempt at self-satisfaction. The first seems good to eat; it also brings the promise that we shall be as God (Gen. 3:5–6). It is not enough, therefore that I seek to walk in the middle path – the path of discipline – nor is my need for a teacher who will teach that path. My need rather is for a saviour who will do for me what I cannot do for myself, who will take away from me that twist in my nature so that I can come to live naturally and spontaneously in God. It is I who am the problem and not the world; it is my Doha and not the world's Dukkha that needs primary solution.[5]

The divergence at this point can be clearly seen. Both Christianity and Buddhism demand the suppression of *selfishness*, but Buddhism goes one step further and demands the suppression of *self*. In the one, the true self is elevated and intensified, in the other, the true self, the illusion of personal individuality, is annihilated. For both, this will lead to the necessity of 'deliverance' or 'liberation'. Both believe that *dukkha* and *doha* can and must be overcome. The Christian believes that human beings have been 'infected' by *doha*, and thus need 'de-contamination', theologically termed 'cleansing' or 'forgiveness'; this they cannot do for themselves and there is only one way to be delivered. For the Buddhist, most disciples must depend upon themselves alone, but much will depend upon which school is followed, because there are different routes that lead to liberation.

The Nature of Deliverance

For some Buddhists, 'ignorance' is understood to be the cause of 'attachment', which leads to evil. Deliverance is by meditation (*wipassana*). To comprehend the real nature of things, one must become 'detached' from ignorance, this will eventually lead to enlightenment. Total commitment to this mental process often leads to mystical experiences. Such 'knowledge' is the beginning of a process which moves from the intellectual to the existential. King perceives that: 'The merely intellectual must penetrate below the cerebral to the visceral level of man's life and awareness: it must cease to be another's deliverance to us, even though it is the Buddha's, and become our own insight. It must be a full, firsthand, "felt-in-the-bones" kind of thing out of which attitude and action will flow.'[6]

Other Buddhist schools see not *ignorance* but *desire* as the root of suffering. Liberation comes through the gradual destruction of desire by the same process, detachment. Everything depends upon total abandonment by the individual in a continual concerted effort to extinguish the fires of desire. The Buddhist Scriptures state: 'Evil is done by self alone, by self alone is one stained; by self alone is evil undone, by self alone is one purified. Purity and impurity depend on one's own self. No man can purify another.'[7] All Buddhists are familiar with a favourite quotation from Gotama: '*A man can depend upon no one except himself.*'

The Means of Deliverance

Following the Eightfold Path should lead to deliverance. Like a soiled white cloth that needs restoring to its original condition, adherence to the Eightfold Path is meant to act as a cleansing agent. Added to this will be the 'teaching' (*Dharma*), likened to a dye which, when added to the cloth, makes it a new colour. A comprehensive knowledge of *Dharma*, the Laws of Buddhism, is essential since this is the way to deliverance.

The ordinary monk is obliged to adhere to 227 different regulations. These cover every aspect of living, from begging for food to sleeping, *ad infinitum*. The standard of perfection demanded in Theravada Buddhism is called *barami*. There are in all thirty categories, each with ten subdivisions, arranged in ascending order of moral difficulty. The Buddha himself had to practise these thirty stages of moral achievement before he could achieve the experience of enlightenment.

In spite of the various standards or levels of achievement indicated in the *Dharma*, Buddhists do not agree on the exact standard which would assure release; they speak of different levels. The height to which one must 'ascend' in order to achieve 'deliverance' is not stated, but most concede that it is beyond the reach of the vast majority. Some schools teach that women need to be reincarnated as men first, and that men must enter permanently into the order of monks if they are to achieve their goal. Yet even with all this, who knows whether one's good merit is going to outweigh one's bad karma? How many possible reincarnations must one endure before one becomes like the Buddha who apparently underwent 500, in order to accomplish the right condition which would lead to Nirvana?

Because of these facts, there is the danger that the Buddhism taught in certain schools may tend to engender fatalism, indifference and hopelessness. Any vestige of hope that there may be will arise from investing in a mountain of good deeds, which must outweigh the bad ones. 'If you do good, you get good and if you do bad, you will receive bad' is a favourite saying of Buddhist people.

Lynn A. de Silva, describing Buddhism, emphasises: 'Buddhism is emphatic in denying the self, and is equally emphatic in affirming the sufficiency of the self in working out his own destiny. In effect Buddhism says "man is nothing, but man alone can do something to determine his own destiny".'[8]

The Agent of Deliverance

In Buddhism the agent of deliverance is one's self, but in Christianity the agent can only be a saviour. Mahayana Buddhism, however, allows for Bodhisattvas (enlightened beings who remain on earth to help others), who can give aid and merit to those who pray to them and follow their teachings. In this case, attainment is not solely dependent on one's own merit alone, but the self-sacrifice of the Bodhisattvas, who postpone their own entrance into Nirvana in order to transfer merit to their devotees.

Some Christians have used the Bodhisattva model as a point of contact to illustrate Christ's willingness to live down here on earth, and offer himself as the ultimate sacrifice for others. The obvious problem is that Christ in the Bible never teaches that he was the end process of almost endless evolutionary reincarnations. He came from heaven once, lived one life and returned to heaven once.

Doubtless, many Buddhists regard the Buddha as a type of glorified Bodhisattva, a god who is alive, who knows all, and hears their prayers − a saviour. Yet the Buddha never claimed to be able to help others, except by means of pointing the way.

The starkest contrast of the two systems centres on the persons of Jesus and Gotama themselves. The central symbol of Christianity is the cross which speaks of God's *involvement in* and *attachment to* the lives of men and women. Christianity unashamedly speaks of establishing the kingdom of God here and now, on earth. The prayer

Christ taught his disciples focuses upon this point: 'Thy kingdom come, Thy will be done on earth as it is in heaven.' His was *a renunciation by involvement* (attachment).

This sharply contrasts with the symbol of Buddhism, a man sitting with legs crossed, withdrawn into imperturbable inner calm, sitting under the Bo tree – a picture of total detachment. The contrast is seen clearly between a way of total involvement in human suffering and sorrow by one person, who taught his followers to be salt and light *in the world*. The Buddha, in contrast, taught his followers a way of escape *from the world*. This is in essence the goal of Buddhism – the resolution of the problem of selfhood by escaping from selfhood.

What is 'selfhood' in Christian teaching? Christian 'deliverance' is not the annihilation of self, but freedom from selfishness. How different this is from the Buddhist idea of 'non-selfhood'. The Buddhist makes relentless war on the self in all its conceptions, forms and manifestations. It is not possible to defeat self by treating the symptoms of the disease, that is by exhortations to be unselfish, to consider others, or by trying to limit self-centredness. The final goal, the only way out, for the human self, or not-self, is the total extinction of the factors that constitute 'human-being'. King describes this as:

An absolute negativity in its every context: metaphysically there is no self, only a temporary collection of elements about the persistent karmic impulse, cemented to it by the glue of ignorance. Religiously speaking, every effort must be bent toward the destruction of self or of the illusion of self, both with regard to intellectual belief in it and the emotional attachment to it. In the end my anatta is to find its terminal home in the final dissolution into nothingness of that fitful, feverish, dream existence sometimes called Life. Is this, then, the end of the doctrine of Buddhist selflessness? In terms of explicit doctrinal statement and religious discipline in the Southern tradition, it *is* the final word.

As such it represents what is perhaps the most baffling form of that negativity so characteristic of Southern Buddhism. It is perhaps the extremist form of the *via negativa* to be found in all the world's religions. And it becomes the more baffling as we try to relate it to a way of ultimate salvation embraced by millions of people. Part of this bafflement is only on paper, since most of these many millions practically speaking *deny* the denial of self by immersing themselves in the pursuit of better self-rebirths and by consoling themselves with the fellowship of the devas and a personalised and living Buddha. But there still remains the problem of the orthodox *via negavita* of anatta, which leads somehow to a joyous and ardently desired salvation.[9]

Whereas the Buddhist tries to disavow self and negate its importance, the Christian can enjoy God and His creation to the full, as well as celebrate, apart from the dark side, his selfhood. Cragg goes as far as affirming that even 'desire', the whole root and cause of *dukkha* can, if perceived correctly, be a positive rather than negative attribute:

> That we can be rightly desirous, is then, the affirmation and the enterprise of the Christian gospel. We leave with a conclusion identifying 'desire', not as the arch-villain, the lurking deceiver, the sure falsifier of the self, but as the quality which authenticates and fulfils it. In so identifying 'desire', we must be clear about the 'desire' we identify. It must be a 'will for which "I" is in no respect a goal', in order that the 'I' may be in every respect a servant, possessed in dispossession.[10]

Christians should not paint too optimistic a picture of self, for there is the 'dark side of self' (lower nature) which must be dealt with. This self from the Christian view still needs a liberator because it is equally a slave to *dukkha* and *doha*. The liberation, however, is not that of extinction or annihilation, but transformation. It is analogous to the metamorphosis of a butterfly, no longer constricted by a hardening chrysalis of selfishness, nor relegated to oblivion, but released to embrace and express in itself the wonder of all that it means to be a 'new creature'.

Before the biblical 'fall', original human beings in their primal innocence were understood to be without *dukkha* or *doha*, being 'created in the image of God'. That image, however, is now shattered, barely reflecting its original image, fragmented, like the shattered windscreen of a car. This 'humpty dumpty', incapable of 'putting itself together again', finds no help 'from all the king's horses and all the king's men'. Only the king can put him together again. This is the essence of Christianity, human beings fallen apart, totally unable to put themselves together again, on the one hand, and God, totally able and willing to restore them to their original image and purpose, on the other.

Christianity recognises primarily, that human beings are no more able to liberate themselves than prisoners can, for if self-liberation were possible they would no longer be prisoners. The very condition they are in reveals first they are not liberated, and second they cannot liberate themselves – the key to the prison door is not in the hands of the prisoners. Human beings are incapable of helping themselves. To tell a terminally ill patient that his only hope is for him to operate on himself would be 'bad news'. The Christian 'good news' is that an expert Surgeon is at hand, ready to give assistance to those who are prepared to put their trust in him. However spiritually ill a person may be the cure is in the hands of another. But even he will not initiate any operation unless he is invited.

This does not mean that Buddhism has no liberator, for there is clearly in Buddhist prophecy the promise of one to come, a deliverer. This hope, however, is for the distant future and gives little comfort for the present. Now, since individuals determine their own salvation, they have no reason to complain about their own present condition, for they are its cause and its effect. No one else can determine the future, for an individual is both its cause and effect – merely reaping the sum total of all the merits or demerits of previous existence. There is however a hint of vicarious suffering in some expressions of Buddhism.

Christmas Humphries suggests that the true Bodhisattva does not suffer for himself, but 'suffers with' humankind:

> Our own pain we just suffer, learning to remove the constant cause of it, the desire of self for self. But others' suffering is more and more our personal concern, and it is a fact to be faced that as we climb the ladder of self-expansion and self-elimination we suffer not less but more. For as we increasingly become aware of the One Life breathing in each brother form of life we learn the meaning of compassion which literally means 'to suffer with'. Henceforth the suffering of all mankind is daily ours, and as the sense of oneness grows so does the awareness of 'that mighty sea of sorrow formed of the tears of men'. Here is the glory of the Bodhisattva ideal, to turn aside at the entrance of Nirvana, and to postpone that ultimate guardian of a thousand lives of effort 'until each blade of grass has entered into Enlightenment'.[11]

There are two problems here. First, in Theravada Buddhism there are no Bodhisattvas, and second, the process of waiting for 'a thousand lives' in order to help others, is for the masses a dim prospect indeed. This truth, of a saviour and substitute, although not so evident in Theravada Buddhism is very clear in Mahayana, where the Bodhisattva is believed to take different bodily forms in order to be able to save. A Bodhisattva resolves:

> I take upon myself the burden of all suffering. I am resolved to do so, I will endure it . . . I must rescue all beings from the stream of *samsara*, which is difficult to cross . . . I myself must grapple with the whole mass of suffering of all beings. To the limit of my endurance I will experience in all the states of woe, found in my world system: all the abodes of suffering.[12]

In response to this identification with humanity's plight,

Mahayana Buddhists see a Bodhisattva as one who is dependable, able to help, and therefore willingly cast their lot with that Bhodhisattva and affirm:

> I believe in him as the highest being: because of the sinfulness of men and because of their suffering, Amida Buddha was incarnate and came upon earth to save men: and only in his suffering love is hope to be found for me and for the world. He became human to become its saviour, and no one but he alone can help. He watches constantly over all who trust in him and helps them.[13]

The idea of substitution, merit-making on behalf of another is common to many religions. In fact most religions require the guilty one to transfer their guilt to another by means of a ritual of substitution. The 'banana leaf float' ceremony in many countries in Asia incorporates this concept. Once a year, there is a 'house cleaning ceremony', then in the evening the whole village will proceed to the local river with a banana leaf float and each person will vicariously place upon the float, all the uncleanness of house and heart, and believe that it will be taken away down river as the float disappears. For example the Thai expression, 'a goat which "takes away" sin' also intimates sin being taken away through the blood of an animal being shed in place of the person concerned. In Tibetan Buddhism there is an actual 'scape-goat ritual'. A goat is selected and symbolically 'loaded with guilt', and then sent out to be killed by whoever finds it.[14]

It seems paradoxical if one applies the folk Buddhist interpretation to an event like Christ's death on the cross. Such an ignominious death is not perceived as a voluntary, self-sacrificial deed, nor is it seen as an example of heroism. It is rather seen as the just retribution of karmic causation. Christ's horrific torturous death could only mean one thing, that in his previous existence he must have been a very wicked person to have acquired such bad karma.

Certain legends and histories in Buddhism do record the concept of sacrificing for others where one person has voluntarily died in place of another. George Appleton points out:

> Buddhism knows much of sacrifice for others, both in the conception of the Bodhi-sat in Northern Buddhism who defers his entry into Nirvana for the sake of men and in the spiritual fables of the Jatakas, the Birth Stories, which picture often in a childlike way, but sometimes with telling maturity, the sacrifices undergone by the Buddha in earlier lives. Neither Bodhisatts – nor Jatakas may be historical, but they are evidence of a conviction within Buddhism that a sacrifice is both right and effective.[15]

One famous historical record of a vicarious substitutionary death was that of Queen Srisuriyothai of Thailand.

> At the time of Burma's first attack against Thailand, the Thai having prepared elephants for combat, sent their king to the front to engage in hand-to-hand combat with the leader of the opposing army. The elephants were used as battering rams. The side whose king was killed would not have the heart to fight on and would flee. In the case of Thailand, if the Thai king was killed it was the equivalent of taking Thailand. On this occasion, the battle lines were set up. King Chakraphat and his two sons rode out on elephants to the battle. Queen Srisuriyothai and her two daughters disguised themselves as men and went out to the battle too. They were dressed exactly the same as the men and rode on elephants in order to witness the battle. When the elephant of King Chakraphat and the elephant of the Burmese general were head-on, in the way that is often portrayed in pictures, and Thai teak models, the Thai elephant was seen to be in the losing position – it was lower than the Burmese elephant. This put the Burmese general in the position in which he could bring his sword down on King Chakraphat. When Queen Srisuriyothai saw what was happening, she quickly drove her

elephant between the two fighting elephants, received the sword blow herself instead of the King. She did this because she knew if the King were killed the country would be lost. This heroic deed showed that she willingly sacrificed her life for the King and her country. A memorial chedi was built to commemorate Queen Srisuriyothai's heroic deed.[16]

In this instance the Queen willingly sacrificed her life in order that her whole country could be saved.

Asian people understand the concept of martyrdom, especially in regard to their soldiers who risk their lives and die – on behalf of the nation. No matter how horrific the circumstances may have been, their deaths are extolled as being the ultimate in self-sacrificial bravery and explained as substitutionary. Such deaths are not interpreted in the folk fashion, as being the result of karmic predestination. They are on the contrary termed 'heroes' – those who died sacrificially on behalf of others. These ideas of substitution, vicarious suffering, of liberation through the intervention of and alleviation by another, are both attractive to the Buddhist and yet at the same time are abhorrent. They undermine the idea of self-determinism, fatalism and karma.

The question of karma raises certain philosophical quandaries. If it is inevitable that people reap now what they have done in the past, why do evil people prosper in the here and now? It could be rationalised that their evil has not yet 'come to fruition'. Does this mean that karma is arbitrary in its timing? Does it also mean that someone with good karma now can suddenly be caught by a dose of bad karma from the past?

Karma can be compared to a super-efficient computer with a memory bank which registers every good and bad thought and deed. It is capable of giving an immediate karmic read-out of the present state of balance in any person's spiritual merit-demerit bank account. The problem is, that at any moment a delayed reading from the memory banks can 'kick in' bringing a karmic updating to the present read out. This could suddenly transform one's 'healthy current account' to being severely overdrawn. So theoretically one could be experiencing a prosperous happy life based on what is perceived to be a good merit build-up in the account, but this may be only because the karmic computer reading has not yet provided the cumulative register of merit versus demerit from past reincarnations and any moment the state of affairs could change. What a terrifying, unreliable, and uncertain state in which to exist. 'Even an evil-doer sees happiness as long as his evil deed has not ripened: but when his evil deed has ripened, then does the evil doer see evil. Even a good man sees evil as long as his good deed has not ripened: but when his good deed has ripened; then does the good man see happiness.'[17]

The uncertainty engendered by this state of affairs, where the predictable karmic read-out, the 'cause and effect' syndrome can no longer be reliable or taken 'as read', will lead to a situation where no judgment can be given regarding any particular condition one is experiencing in this life. In other words, it is impossible to take one's present situation for granted. If people really accepted the principle of the unreliability of karma, there could be no value judgments on anybody as they are at present. However, in actual fact, all Buddhists do make value judgments about the state of the person in the present, based upon whether they are receiving what appears to be 'good fortune' (health, wealth and prosperity) or conversely, 'bad fortune'. Karmic read-outs become totally unreliable and there can no longer be any certainty with regard to the law of cause and effect.

In effect a Buddhist should never make a value judgment on other human beings since at any moment the karma principle could 'kick in' and reveal a totally different state of affairs. What one may end up with is a possible situation in which, because present circumstances appear to be 'propitious', a person may justifiably feel they are enjoying the rewards of good karma; only to be suddenly hit with a massive application of destructive karma. In other words, all the merit gained could be wiped out in a flash, like the Wall Street Crash, leaving the victim spiritually bankrupt. In which case the next life must mean the inevitability of being reborn to a lower status other than a rational human being, destined to a sub-human existence, no longer capable of informed decisions or moral choices, but just driven by base animal instinct.

Since the karmic principle for human beings is always based on moral behaviour (the choice of good or bad), built up from previous lives, how does one apply such a principle to animals who can hardly be judged as having moral/ethical capability? How can a mosquito, or a mouse gain merit or demerit if it is acquired through making a series of responsible or even irresponsible choices?

The nature of 'accidents' also demands attention, and they are frequent enough everywhere. Are they really 'accidents', or is there some form of 'predestination' governed by karmic force? Does a person's present condition always depend upon their good or bad karma? What about war, or natural disasters, when thousands of people may be suddenly engulfed in a similar catastrophe, so that each person suffers exactly the same fate? Have they all behaved in exactly the same way in their previous existence, so as to experience the same catastrophic 'fate' now? What about 'the killing fields'? What about Auschwitz, or Belsen, or Hiroshima? Can one reasonably apply the law of karma to these scenes of devastation? Does one have to assume that none of the victims was innocent, but they had all committed exactly the same degree of sin, so as to deserve exactly the same degree of punishment?

Christmas Humphries, the spokesman for Western-style Buddhism, ingeniously borrows the Good Samaritan story of the New Testament and attempts to convince his readers that:

The Good Samaritan of the Christian New Testament was not 'interfering' with the karma of him he helped, while he that passed by suffered the grave loss of an opportunity. It is your karma that *you* should be helped, as you are, or left unaided as you may be, and it is your friend's good karma to have you as his friend. Away then with all thoughts of interference . . . The avalanche which sweeps down the mountain cannot be stayed. Such karma is 'ripe' for reception, and no new cause of our devising can stay the conclusion of cause-effect. Such karma has the force of destiny, of fate, all else is unchangeable.[18]

To borrow his own analogy, but not using just one 'good Samaritan' one may ask, what if the avalanche he speaks of sweeps down a mountain and engulfs a whole township? Do all those victims in the town deserve the same 'force of destiny' predicated by karma? Were they all equally bad?

Humphries also assumes that in all conditions, *we* can and must be in charge of our own fate. He explains that while one cannot stop it raining, one can control one's physical, emotional and mental reaction to the fact of rain.[19] Is one also supposed to be able to control one's physical, emotional and mental reaction if an avalanche is descending? Such assumptions may work when related to rain, but what about the problem of pain? Does karma predetermine the way our characters are formed? Is no one to blame except ourselves, both in the past and the present? Humphries again speaks clearly of the Buddhist hope when he states:

Is a picture of Buddhist values beginning to emerge? No God, no Saviour, but every man a busy gardener removing weeds and cultivating virtues; or to change the simile, concerned with the purification and the expansion of his own consciousness, until like that of the Buddha, it is commensurate with the universe. None can hurry the pilgrim on his Way, none can prevent his reaching the goal.[20]

To be able to attain to such heights of 'expansion of one's

own consciousness', in order to be reborn at a higher level in the future, requires a total abandonment of the natural way of living, such as enjoying the beauty of creation, music, art, friendships, the love of family and children. The stakes have proved to be too high for many Buddhists. The Christian, on the other hand, can gladly accept all these without reservation as God-given virtues. It is no wonder that the most devout Buddhist sometimes asks – is it really worth it?

It is at this point that the fact of liberation, deliverance or extrication by another comes as sweet music to the ear. The good news is that, ontologically, and existentially it is possible for karma to be cheated of its prey, for people to be delivered from its clutch.

Usually karma is seen from a negative perspective: 'It is said that acts of hatred and violence tend to lead to rebirth in a hell, acts bound up with delusion and confusion tend to lead to rebirth as an animal, and acts of greed tend to lead to rebirth as a ghost.'[21] But let us not forget the possibility of accruing 'good karma'. Whatever good is experienced now, is viewed as being the result of good karma from a previous existence. It is quite understandable to speak in terms of *humans* gaining a higher degree of merit and progress towards enlightenment if such advancement relates to a series of moral choices resulting in good moral behaviour. But one is obliged to ask again, how can animals possibly progress in the same way? Reincarnation predicates the possibility of intelligence and choice in a moral sense. To reiterate, one would question whether a cockroach, cat, or camel, has the capability of moral choice, the intelligence, or even the will to progress up the ladder? Can (or must), an animal ascend to human-hood, before it is able to reach its ultimate goal of Nirvana? And why is it that (as some believe) a woman must be reincarnated into a man as the next step up the ladder to any advancement? If the law of karma is just, then there must surely be equal opportunities for all to gain merit, which in turn would presuppose equal capability to make the choices essential to progress. But what chances can animals have in contrast to humans, or even women in contrast to men? It has been suggested these questions reveal massive 'black holes' of philosophical inconsistency, injustice and gender prejudice. Conversely, we may just have to accept that the qualifications or conditions regarding rebirth are simply unknown, that 'ignorance' (*avija*), prevails. But if that is the case how can one base a philosophy or belief system on 'ignorance', that which we do not know?

Good karma has been interpreted at three levels. The folk level regards it as 'well-being' and prosperity, which would include having all the benefits of materialism. At a slightly more sophisticated level, ordinary Buddhism would see it as possessing the positive qualities of an individual, in terms of achieving inner peace, equanimity or detachment. Philosophical Buddhism cannot define what exactly good karma is, unless it is just 'an echo', that is passed on from one existence to another. They believe there is no immortal soul or self that persists from one rebirth to another. Even those immaterial factors (the decision making capacities and the function of the mind), which compose the mental or spiritual side of human beings, will dissolve. King tries to explain:

> The whole structure called 'a person' simply falls apart upon death, yet this falling apart is perhaps not simple. For the force of its falling produces at least an echo as it were. Indeed it is more than a mere echo. It is in some sense the continuation of this structure that was a self or person, and results in a new self, or at least sentient being of some sort. What the nature of this ongoing impulse is in actuality raises a considerable philosophical problem. We shall only note the orthodox Buddhist answer to those who persist in perplexity 'that which passes on from one birth to another is not identical with self. Indeed, what passes on even from one moment of our present existence to the next is not the same in terms of identity.' The following analogies are often used to illustrate this different but connected

relationship: milk changes to curds to cheese: a tree produces a seed that produces a tree of the same kind, that produces a seed – and so on ad infinitum. Or we may quote a direct answer to the same question in more philosophical language: 'If there is no Atta, the self or soul, what is it that moves from life to life, changing all the time until it enters into the state of Nirvana, which is the only unchanging Reality?' The answer is the uninterrupted process of psychophysical phenomena or the composition of the five aggregates which is called a being.[22]

All three viewpoints at least accept the extent to which one had refrained from evil, done good, and purified one's heart (which is the sum of Buddhism); to that extent one will be credited with good karma. Just how this transference is accomplished, between whom and the time span between the transfer raises unanswerable questions. Behind the three viewpoints is the general assurance that merit can and will be transferred, to 'top up' that which might be needed for a better rebirth.

In fact the whole order of the priesthood is based on the presupposition that it is possible to *transfer* good karma. Even in Theravada Buddhism, all young boys are pressured to go into the priesthood, not for their own benefit or on their own behalf, but for their parents. This is 'paying back the cost of mother's milk', Wan elaborates:

Those who enter the priesthood today have only one idea in mind, to repay their parents. In Thai custom it is felt that if one has a son, he brings much merit (boon), and when that son goes into the priesthood, they feel that if the mother has committed any sins, by virtue of the son's priesthood, when she dies she may 'go to heaven on yellow cloth'. She goes to heaven on the merit of her son. There are many stories about this.[23]

Wan further intimates that there are many reasons for entering the priesthood, some because of unemployment, some illness, some old age, some sincerely believe that it is a step on the way to Nirvana. 'But most today enter the priesthood because of custom. If we ask why they do it, most would answer, "My parents have brought me up. I want to repay them. They want me to do it and I am doing it for them".'[24]

Thus the concept of the transference of merit from one person to another is wholly acceptable within a Buddhist world-view. It covers transference *from* those already departed, to those living now; it includes transference *between* living persons; it even includes transference *by* people living now back *to* ancestors, or recently departed members of the family. The concept of transference from the Bodhisattva or from the Buddha himself to another undeserving person, is a belief deeply ingrained in the Buddhist psyche.

Interestingly enough, even folk Buddhism believes that there is a way to short circuit, or 'deactivate' karma. The process of nullifying or deactivating karma can actually happen if and when one is prepared 'to ask forgiveness'. Although this petition is sometimes addressed to fellow human beings, it is often addressed 'into the air' in the hope that Someone 'out there' will hear and forgive.

Enlightenment and Nirvana

Gotama's experience of enlightenment is the basic foundation of Buddhism. While seated under the now famous Bo tree, a poplar-fig tree, he began to dilate, closing the eyes and heart from all distractions until he was finally unaware of sound, taste, touch or sensation. With his spiritual perception heightened, he began to strip off layer after layer of the nature of existence until he 'saw' and was enlightened – which means 'to know'. Wan defines the process in this way:

When Lord Buddha was enlightened he did not study from anyone else. First he practised concentration according to the accepted method. Those who practised it sat quietly, did not even so much as blink, held their tongues firmly to the roof of their mouths, scarcely breathed, folded their hands until they nearly grew together. We can almost say that they tortured themselves. Lord Buddha tried this for six years without success and eventually gave it up. Finally he turned to the use of the mind and was able to solve the problem through thought. At last he knew the 'truth' about life. This experience of his is called 'enlightenment'. He learned three truths which are considered the highest wisdom in Buddhism:

1. He knew about his own previous reincarnations. According to one account he saw that he had been reincarnated five hundred times, sometimes as a monkey, sometimes as a dog, a bird, a cat, a mouse and in many tens of other ways. But gradually in these rebirths he advanced until he became Lord Buddha.

2. He was enlightened to the births and deaths of others, together with the dates of births and deaths. This ability is called the Celestial Eye.

3. He knew himself to be emancipated from ignorance and from the cycle of rebirths. He had been enlightened.[25]

Some Christians have wrongly attempted to use this concept of enlightenment to explain the nature of Christian conversion or even assert that Christ, like the Buddha, also needed to be enlightened. But this is so much in contrast to Humphries, an authoritative interpreter, who in explaining the essence of conversion in Buddhism, reveals clearly its nature and source:

In the absence of a mighty Being who has power to withhold the sequence of cause-effect the Buddhist looks within for his spiritual needs, including his 'salvation'. He is therefore at the outset of his religious life thrown back on his own interior sources: for him the Buddha is never more, though never less, than a Guide and Leader on the Way... the essence of conversion is in the turning. Psychologically it is a process of intro-version, or turning inward, a withdrawal of consciousness from the phenomenal world into the noumenal Essence of Mind which is the highest cognisable reality.[26]

The Nature of Nirvana

The subject of comparing the Buddhist *Nirvana* with the Christian concept of heaven is a matter for continual debate. The debate revolves around semantics, a constant problem due to the danger of using Buddhist terminology for Christian concepts and vice versa.

Nirvana for the Buddhist is described not as a place, but as a state of being, or perhaps a state of non-being. To be in Nirvana is literally to be extinguished. There will be no birth, or re-birth, no attachment, no desire, no ignorance, no passion or anger, nothing. Nirvana is not a place, it is a 'stateless-state', an unreal reality. Saddhatissa describes it thus:

> Nirvana defies description . . . it has been called the deathless, the other shore, being uncompounded, it is not subject to the three characteristics of compounded things, impermanence (*dukka*) and substance less. It is compared to the wind, it is made of nothing at all. One cannot say of Nirvana that it arises or that it does not arise, or that it is to be produced or that it is past or future or present, that is is cognisable, by the eye, ear, nose, tongue or body.[27]

The average Buddhist, however, has no real aspiration to reach Nirvana, because it is generally accepted to belong only to those devotees already ordained into the priesthood, who spend all their time in meditation and good works of merit. In popular Buddhism there is another place called 'heaven' (*sawan*). This is an intermediate state between death and Nirvana in which there are apparently various levels of bliss as there are various levels of hell, with increasingly intense experiences or levels of torment. The good side of this 'heaven' is naturally more attractive since it is at least attainable by the layperson. Dr Kenneth Wells in describing the funeral rites for an average Buddhist explains beliefs regarding those recently departed:

> There is an underlying mood of resignation to funerals: among a choice few there is the hope of Nirvana with the extinction of personal striving: among the vast majority there is the expectation of rebirth, either in this world, in the heaven of Indra or some other, or in another plane of existence, possibly as a spirit. Over the basic mood of gloom there has grown up a feeling that meritorious acts and the grace of the Lord Buddha can aid the condition of the departed.[28]

Folk Buddhism therefore offers a more realistic hope with the aid of the Lord Buddha, than Nirvana. Thomas Kirsch points out that there is this great gulf between the orthodox belief in Nirvana, and Folk Buddhism:

> There is a special problem. The outline of Buddhism which I have presented is derived basically from their formal belief system and carried by religious virtuosos, e.g., the monks. But few laymen are so sophisticated as monks in terms of either their religious belief or practices. For example the religiously sophisticated may pursue the abstract religious goal of nirvana. When queried most laymen view the goal of their Buddhist religious actions to be a sojourn in 'paradise' (sawan). Lay Buddhists may be recognising a point which sophisticated doctrine makes explicit: that nirvana is extremely difficult for any one to achieve. Only those with especially favourable moral balances may realistically aspire to achievement of that ultimate goal. Hence the layman focuses on more immediate and attainable goals.[29]

By comparison, the Christian gospel has much to offer at

this point. It may certainly be termed 'good news' for those who live with such unrealisable and unachievable aspirations. Heaven for the Christian is not reserved for the elite, or even for the minority, it is 'prepared' for all those who put their trust in Christ. It is one of the 'givens' of Christianity, granted by the grace of the one who was both qualified (as King) and able (as Redeemer).

Hope for the Christian's future is portrayed by a picture of a great multitude of people, worshipping Christ around his throne (Revelation chapter 7), described as people from 'every nation, tribe, people and language'. Heaven therefore, is not perceived merely as a 'state of being', it is necessarily a physical place – 'to be with Christ'. The biblical view of heaven cannot imply merely a state of mind, or annihilation. John records Christ's repeated assurances to his disciples that 'where I am you will be also' (John 14:1).

For the Christian attaining heaven is unembarrassedly a condition of joy, peace, harmony, love, worship, recognition and community, a far more attractive prospect than achieving Nirvana and becoming a single drop of dew dissolving into an ocean of nothingness; a complete evaporation of whoever I was and whoever I would like to have been.

1. B. H. Streeter, *The Buddha and the Christ* (Macmillan, 1932), p. 63.
2. Winston King, *Buddhism and Christianity* (Allen & Unwin, 1963), p. 115.
3. Ibid., p. 115.
4. Ibid.
5. D. T. Niles, *Buddhism and the Claims of Christ* (Knox, 1967), p. 49.
6. King, *Buddhism and Christianity*, p. 128.
7. E. Conze (ed.) *Buddhist Scriptures* (Penguin Classics, 1969), p. 62.
8. Lynn A. de Silva, *Creation, Redemption, Consummation* (Sinclair Thompson Memorial Lectures series 3, Chiengmai, Thailand, 1964), p. 69.

9. Kenneth Cragg, *The Christ and the Faiths* (SPCK, 1986), p. 263.

10. Ibid., p. 265.

11. Christmas Humphries, *Buddhism* (Penguin Books, 1951), p. 53.

12. De Silva, *Creation, Redemption, Consummation*, p. 69.

13. Ibid., p. 70.

14. Marku Tsering, Sharing Christ in the Tibetan Buddhist World (Tibet Press, 1988), p. 108.

15. George Appleton, *Christian Presence and Buddhism* (SCM Press, 1961), p. 51.

16. De Silva, *Creation, Redemptiom, Consummation*, p. 73.

17. Christmas Humphries, *The Buddhist Way of Life* (Allen & Unwin, 1969), p. 85.

18. J. Davis, *Poles Apart* (ATA Books, 1993), p. 72.

19. Humphries, *The Buddhist Way of Life*, p. 143.

20. Ibid., p. 85.

21. Peter Harvey, *An Introduction to Buddhism* (Cambridge University Press, 1990), p. 39.

22. King, *Buddhism and Christianity*, p. 192.

23. Wan Pettsongkhram, *Talks in the Shade of the Bo Tree* (Thai Gospel Press, 1975), p. 20.

24. Ibid., p. 93.

25. Ibid.

26. Humphries, *The Buddhist Way of Life*, p. 114.

27. H. Saddhatissa, *The Buddha's Way* (Allen & Unwin, 1971), p. 42.

28. Kenneth Wells, *Thai Buddhism: the History of Protestant Work in Thailand 1825–1958* (Bangkok Church of Christ, 1958), p. 214.

29. Thomas Kirsch, *Clues to Thai Culture* (OMF Publishers, Bangkok, 1973), p. 125.

5

Spirituality and Worship – Public and Private Devotion

While there are obviously a number of significant doctrinal differences between the various Buddhist schools, concerning for instance, the distinguishing features and role of the Bodhisattvas, or the nature of 'personhood' (*atman*), there is nevertheless one prevalent thread, a *sine qua non* of all Buddhist expressions of faith and that is a common aspiration for, and progression towards what may be termed 'spirituality'. This concept is difficult to define and various terminologies have been used to explain its meaning; such as 'deep insight', 'equanimity', 'tranquillity', 'detachment', 'the illumination of wisdom', or even 'enlightenment'. However, put simply it means that devotees are intent upon attaining a level of 'awareness' and 'beingness' that far exceeds the normal quality of life experienced by the average Buddhist.

There are of course paradoxes to be faced when one considers how one advances towards or attains 'spirituality'. Should one *determine* to reach prescribed goals? Or should one have no goals at all? If all *desire* is essentially wrong, how can it be right that one should vigorously *desire* 'spirituality'? Kornfield tries to explain this paradox when he states:

> Strive very hard to achieve concentration of mind . . . you are extremely fortunate to be born a human and to hear the Dharma. Don't waste this chance. Work, meditate vigorously. This is one approach. In the second

approach, there is nothing to gain, nowhere to go. The very effort you make to be enlightened will prevent wisdom from arising, for *wisdom can never arise from desire*. Simply be, let go and watch. Naturally, right here, right now; that is all there is; striving, not striving; both can bring balance. Eventually, whatever practice one follows *must be let go of, even the practice of letting go!*[1]

In the final analysis the difference between the various schools in their goal to attain 'spirituality' centres on *how* one may attain, rather than *what* is the common goal. All agree, the goal is to be 'released' from all forms of desire, because desire is the root cause of all human suffering.

Various exercises engaged upon for the development of 'spirituality' are all with a view to achieving the one specific goal, which finally leads to the annihilation of individual 'personhood' (*atman*), self-hood, or 'the ego'. This is because the Buddhist believes that the very fact of one's existence is the effective cause of suffering. This is called 'dependent origination'. To use an analogy; as a fishing net is constructed by tying together a series of knots, so everything in this world is made up of a series of connected meshes and we are inexorably caught in this net of 'causes and conditions' by the fact that we exist. Because our very existence predestines us to have *desire* and this results in suffering, then logically, if the desire can be removed – especially our deluded attachment to 'existence' – human suffering will come to an end. So also will human existence. That is after all what the devout follower of the *Dharma* is aiming at; so the beginning of enlightenment is the consequence of the termination of personal existence.

The only effective way to being released from such causes and preconditions is through the development of spirituality (perhaps this should simply be defined as 'the-state-of-no-longer-desiring'). This is attained through almost every imaginable type of stringent exercise that can be conceived.

In Buddhist perception the lotus flower has special

significance. The efforts towards spirituality may be compared to the idea of applying fertiliser to a lotus flower which grows out of mud in a swamp, so that emerging from the surrounding muck of worldly passions will spring a beautiful flower of spirituality, blossoming to enlightenment. Here the 'muck' or mud can be compared to our physical body; the emerging lotus flower can be compared to the developing (budding) perceptions of our minds. The 'fertilising' relates to the direct application of exercise to the goal in view. The fully opened lotus would be the full expression of the Buddha-mind now visible as a beautiful lotus flower in full bloom.

Another illustration is that if a king was plagued by bandits, he would need to ascertain where their camp was before he could be rid of them. Likewise in the development of spirituality, one must discover and pursue, at all costs, those factors which impede and obstruct spiritual progress. The disturbances and defilements of our thinking processes need to be identified and dealt with, and this can only be effected by developing equanimity of mind through exercises which will lead to spirituality.

Right mindfulness (*Samma-sati*) is the essential ingredient to accelerated development along the path to spirituality. This, combined with correct body positions (*Yoga*), should lead to a heightened awareness of mental and physical stimuli. Outwardly, assuming the lotus sitting position, observing the movement of muscles, the sound of breathing, 'feeling' the stillness in the air, concentrating on colour, texture, feeling of objects, all contribute to higher awareness. Inwardly, the various 'states of mind' which encompass the changing quality of the thought processes may be expressed by evidences of enthusiasm, joy, depression, anger, lethargy or any other emotional feeling. All contribute to the development of ever deepening levels of awareness beyond the norm. These exercises lead to 'right effort' which improves perception, intuition and will power. It is necessary to concentrate on *insight* in order to measure accurately the states of mind that emerge especially those which are habitually dominant. These may then be either held on to, or discarded, on the basis of whether they would help, hinder (or even cause to abort) progress along the spiritual journey. It is therefore necessary to develop *intuition* so that one can gauge whether it would be wise or not, to let oneself venture any further into any, as yet unknown state of mind. This leads of course to the necessity of *will power* to be able to say either 'yes' or 'no' to a particular direction one may be journeying along; for some pathways can be dangerous. Thomas Merton explains the pitfalls along this pathway:

> It becomes overwhelmingly important for us to become detached from our everyday conception of ourselves as potential subjects for special and unique experiences, or as candidates for realisation, attainment and fulfilment. In other words, this means that a spiritual guide worth his salt will conduct a ruthless campaign against all forms of delusion arising out of spiritual ambition and self-complacency which aims to establish the ego in spiritual glory. This is why a St John of the Cross is so hostile to visions, ecstasies and all forms of 'special experience'. That is why the Zen Masters say 'If you meet the Buddha, kill him.'[2]

Although cognitive understanding of the middle path is essential to the development of spirituality, this is really only the launching pad from which an ever deepening process is developed, into effective methods of attainment, principally by the use of various forms and means of meditation. Some schools of meditation have developed sophisticated 'tailor made' approaches to the skill, which would be dependent upon the character and temperament of the devotee, or what their dominant quality might be. Six basic behavioural characteristics are predicated, and it would be on the basis of such behavioural tendencies that appropriate methodologies of meditation would be prescribed and practised. The six characteristics are greed, hate, delusion, faith, intelligence and discursiveness.

Interestingly, those who apparently act from faith are, it

is claimed, similar to those who act from greed. For people who are diagnosed as dominated by greed, their faith would be strong because it is understood that the quality of faith is similar to the quality of greed. The obvious inconsistencies and interpretations of what may appear to be contradictory qualities seem to be irrelevant to the Teacher and his devotee.[3] Various manuals may be consulted and personal charts are prescribed which will offer the particular form of meditation appropriate to the particular weakness. So for instance, a person dominated by greed would need to meditate on the ten repulsive aspects of a decomposing corpse. The list is the most gruesome or grotesque picture of rotting flesh, that the details are better not elaborated upon. At times instructions may be given by a more experienced monk to a group that they together meditate on a decaying corpse (duly brought in to the temple grounds for this purpose). This is a form of 'preventative medicine', keeping one from being attracted or attached to the human form with its illusion of beauty.

Following this process of meditation, various levels of attainment are aimed at, which may often lead to one or a number of supernatural experiences. Of these, the 'five miraculous powers' are the most 'desired'. They are experiences of:

1. 'various magical powers';
2. 'cognition by the heavenly ear';
3. 'knowledge of others' thoughts';
4. 'recollection of previous lives';
5. 'knowledge of the decease and rebirth of other beings'.

When put together this imposing list of supernatural abilities produces nothing less than a 'superman'; for even in category one, the person is enabled to become invisible and visible at will, able to walk through walls and glide unimpeded through space; able to dive in and out of the earth; able to walk on water without sinking; able to float along like a bird on wing, while sitting in the lotus position; able to overcome time and space; able to make what is little into what is much; able to metamorphose into any animal, human, or divine being; able to produce 'mind-made bodies'. The last of these is achieved by turning attention to one's own body, and then resolving that there will be a hollow space inside.

> In consequence there is a hollow space. He then thinks attentively of a second body in the hollow space within his own body, makes the necessary preparations, produces a sustained resolve and in consequence there is now within his own body still another body. Hence it is said 'here the monk conjures up from his body another body, which has form, is mind-made, complete with all its limbs, in full possession of its organs'.[4]

The subtle differences or levels between the various forms of meditation are accentuated the deeper the path is followed. These levels are called *yanas* or *jhanas* and they are defined very precisely, so that one will be sharply aware of passing from one level to another by detailed diagnosis of the 'state' one has attained so far. Eventually one will pass from a state of 'infinite consciousness' (that which Thomas Merton would describe as 'super consciousness'), leading on to a state of 'infinite nothingness', which really means the 'termination of all perception and sensation' – this is the penultimate step before one is released into Nirvana.

Such goals raise philosophical and religious questions. Why would any *person* want to be a *non-person*? Why would anyone want to move from a state of awareness of their true 'human-beingness' to a state where all human faculties are suspended, a virtual zombie-like state (by definition, one who thinks or acts mechanically, without intelligence or enjoyment)? Perhaps this is even a contradiction of terms, for even a zombie 'thinks or acts', but this state of non-perception and non-sensation means absolutely, 'nothing' or 'nothingness'. One must also ask, why is the human body perceived as so disgusting that one must meditate on a rotting corpse? What is wrong with 'attachment' to those things in the world that are wholesome, and good? From a Christian perspective, one can embrace with all the vigour of one's being, and rejoice in all the positive dimensions of 'personhood', while at the same time recognising the 'dark side' of human behaviour. One can also enjoy the beauty of the human form in its youthful magnificence, while again recognising that such beauty is 'here today and gone tomorrow'. But so is every bird in the air, every flower of the field or every tree in the forest. Despite their transient nature, they all proclaim ingenious design, creative beauty, artistic imagination, multi-coloured variety. Why not 'get attached' to all of this? Such attachment may even alleviate the inevitable suffering all humanity experiences. The option of Nirvana, a state without suffering, would seem quite unattractive in comparison to embracing the beauty of this world even with its suffering. These theoretical options may be perceived by some to be a caricature of both the concept of attachment and Nirvana, but they are most certainly what the average lay person understands concerning the nature of things.

Wipassana, one of the more sophisticated methods of meditation, is based on the principle of recollection of and concentration on what is termed 'in-breathing and out-breathing'. Attention is focused on the tip of the nostrils, the meditator observes the passage of breath while exhaling and inhaling. This *wipassana*-type meditation demands continual mentoring and analysis. One commentator indicates that *wipassana* demands a ruthless honesty and a deep-rooted conviction that this must be 'the way'. Without such honesty, the mind will avoid the issue and not be able to focus.

Another form, *samantha* or *samati*, seeks to encourage the mind to focus for a prolonged period, in blissful quietness, on a particular object (or objects). Whatever may result from this, whether there are ecstatic 'trances' or terrifying visions, such experiences should be allowed to pass over the person, who should give no reaction, or at the most, just respond with detached equanimity. The outcome of correct meditation will be the development of hitherto unknown 'insights' that are neither learned by the rational mind, nor can be explained in normal terms – they can only be experienced.

Theravada Buddhism stresses 'path consciousness' and that there are four stages along this path that release the chains that keep people in bondage. At each stage, a fetter will be broken until finally at the fourth stage the remnants of ignorance will be uprooted and complete enlightenment result. The *wipassana* and *samati* methods of meditation in the Southern school of Buddhism are at the heart of its teaching, for it is through progressing along this 'pathway' that devotees will pursue complete detachment, and finally arrive at the peak of spirituality, when they will be ready for release into Nirvana.

The school of *Vajrayana* Buddhism – the word originally meant 'Thunderbolt of the god Indra', but came to mean 'the diamond vehicle' – extends to Tibet, China and Japan, and has its own distinctive features in terms of spirituality. It has various ceremonies or rituals where one achieves trance-like states and becomes a medium or mouthpiece of spirits. For instance, after a long 'weeding out process', the selection of a new Dalai Lama is finally determined during this type of ritual, to ascertain confirmation from the gods who really is the genuine reincarnation of the previous Dalai Lama. This school depends very much upon *mantras* and *mudras*, the former being the vocalisation of various strange sounds, and the latter the physical gestures that accompany worship.

Included in these ceremonies are certain well-kept secrets which only the initiated are allowed to experience. At the same time, the school has acquired a very strong erotic element called *Shaktiism*. It engages in public expressions of orgiastic worship which are supposed to join the participants 'to the universal feminine' and so realise the ultimate unity of all things. It need hardly be said that this addition to Buddhism is despised by other stricter movements.[5]

Aids to Worship

Various aids to worship may be used. Different schools will use different mechanisms or objects that will direct one's focus in prayer and worship. It naturally goes without saying that icons, images, idols, pictures, shrines, *yantras* (special symbols or hieroglyphics written on pieces of cloth and hung in all sorts of places including vehicles for protection), all act as foci for the various schools.

The Nichiren Shosu school in Japan focus worship on a black wooden box the *gohonson*. This contains names of famous people taken from the *Lotus Sutra*. The box is reported to contain 'universal forces' that destine or control a disciple's future pathway. One has to kneel before the wooden box, recite passages from the *Lotus Sutra*, rub beads and chant a mantra '*nam-myoho-renegkyo*'. The original box is situated at the foot of Mount Fuji. There are other 'representations' of the box in various temples.

In other schools (especially Tibetan), prayer beads called *malas* are also used. These have 108 beads – an auspicious number which apparently has its origins in ancient Indian astrology. The rosaries assist in remembering the number of prostrations that one should undergo, or a certain number of particular *mantras* that must be chanted. Prayer flags and prayer wheels are used extensively in Tibetan Buddhism. Inscribed on the flags and on the inside or outside of some of the wheels, there will be sets of prayers. The wheels are cylindrical in shape and are spun by the hand as devotees move along the side of temple walls in which the wheels have been installed. Most of the wheels include the inscription '*Om mani padme, hum*' renowned as the most powerful mantra. A literal translation would be:

Om	Hail to the diamond jewel
Mani	of Nirvana in wisdom and compassion
Padme	the lotus which symbolises samsara.
Hum	Welcome

However, these same sounds are interpreted in a completely different way in the book *Religions of the East* where Ann Bancroft suggests:

Om	=	gods
Ma	=	anti-gods
Ni	=	humans
Pad	=	animals
Me	=	*pretas* hungry ghosts
Hum	=	hell

The six syllables are meant to compare with the six worlds of the human mind. Each sound is interpreted to convey a state of human thinking. Bancroft states 'as the syllables of Om Mani Padme Hum are intoned slowly the written form of each syllable is visualised as emitting shining rays of comfort to the beings in each of the six worlds'.[6] Other significant visual aids to worship are *mandalas*. These are detailed pictorial representations of certain cosmic truths portrayed in dramatic colourful form. A wheel or circle will form the basis of most the mandalas. Although there are literally thousands, each telling their own stories, the most famous is the Tibetan 'Wheel of Life' mandala which portrays a rotating wheel, with a monster, Yama, the Lord of Death, wearing a crown of five human skulls. On the outside he is seen to be holding the wheel between two fangs at the top, and gripping it at the sides. Inside the hub of the wheel there are three animals – a cock, representing craving for life, a snake, the embodiment of hatred and enmity and a pig symbolising ignorance. As the wheel turns, each animal appears to devour the tail of the other. Moving from the outside edge to the inside of the picture, both the animals and humans appear to get more and more grotesque with frightening prospects of being tortured or dismembered. There is a vivid picture depicting hell, with hungry ghosts waiting around to devour anything available. The mandala has six sections, at the outer edge of which are twelve figures, each representing the twelve chains which 'bind humans to this life'. Bancroft[7] describes the twelve chains as:

1. A blind man, representing primordial ignorance.
2. A potter, fashioning the first impulses that arise out of ignorance.
3. A monkey playing with a peach. He has become conscious of his impulses as he tastes good and evil.
4. Two men in a boat. The consciousness of personality has arisen, and this led to name and form.
5. Six empty houses, show the six sense perceptions of consciousness (Buddhists include the mind as a sense of perception).
6. A man and a woman in an embrace of love (the senses are now desiring contact with their objects).
7. A man with arrows in both eyes, which are the blind feeling of pleasure and pain.
8. An offering of drink, representing the thirst for existence.
9. A monkey stealing fruit. This is the thirst for existence leading to grasping.
10. A pregnant woman. The greed for life leads to more and more becoming.
11. Childbirth, which represents rebirth.
12. A corpse, which is rebirth giving rise to decay and death and more rebirth in a perpetual round.

Above in the clouds the Buddha is pointing to the Pathway as the only way of liberation.

Corporate Worship

So far the discussion has centred on each individual endeavouring to attain a high level of spirituality. There are also, certain forms of joint activity, which may be termed 'worship' but not if the concept of worship is associated with the word 'God'.

If one uses the word 'worship' in accordance with its

original meaning 'worth-ship', then Buddhists do engage in corporate worship, centred on the *Dharma*, rather than a personal god. Likewise, 'prayer'; if this is not used in terms of beseeching a divine being, but rather in the sense of meditating on one's own inner spiritual journey, then it may also be used.

As indicated already, each temple compound will have a special *wihara* building which is spacious enough to permit a large number of persons to come together, including the monks and the laity, for corporate times of worship.

It is true to say there will be considerable difference between what is believed by the monks and the laity, as worship proceeds and meditation centres on the *Dharma*. Beyond the reading of the *Dharma* the lay people will hope that the Buddha *will* grant merit to them because of the simple fact that they are in attendance, participating in worship. Beyond the *lifeless* image of the Buddha, the laity will be hoping there *is* someone who is still *alive* and listening to their prayers. After all if other divine beings (Bodhisattvas) are able to transfer their merit, commensurate with the good deeds of devotees, and if going to worship is regarded as the highest good deed, then it must surely follow that their Buddha, who is above all the Bodhisattvas, will be equally as generous in extending his merit to them.

While incense, flowers, prostrations and prayers are being offered a joint prayer may be uttered as follows:

Reverencing the Buddha we offer *flowers*,
Flowers that today are fresh and sweetly blooming,
flowers that tomorrow are faded and failed,
Our bodies too like flowers will pass away.

Reverencing the Buddha we offer *candles*
To Him who is the light, we offer light.
From His greater lamp a lesser lamp we light within us
The lamp of Bodhi shining within our hearts.

Reverencing the Buddha we offer *incense*

Incense whose fragrance pervades the air,
The fragrance of the perfect life, sweeter than incense
Spreads in all directions throughout the world.[8]

In the midst of such times of worship, one can see how easy it becomes to slip from loving the *Dharma* and reverencing the Buddha as a past memory, to go one step further and to speak of him (and to him) as though he were still alive; when in actual fact, because he is the Enlightened One, he no longer exists, but has been dissolved into nothingness. For those of the Mahayana tradition, there is a sevenfold devotion which is called *Puja* (worship), commonly used in Hinduism also.

The seven aspects of this devotion are:

1. The prostrations
2. The seven or eight offerings
3. The confession
4. The sense of joy (following confession)
5. The petitioning
6. The request that the Buddhas remain active in the world
7. The giving away of merit

Such petitions and intercession are easier for the Mahayanans because they address their prayers, not only to the Buddha, but to the Bodhisattvas and other divine beings who may be able to help – whoever they are.

It should be remembered that corporate worship is normally quite difficult for those of both Theravada and Mahayana schools to engage in as the monks will, for the most part, be chanting in the original languages. The laity are very much dependent on familiarity of sound because they do not understand the original language. However, this is changing and nowadays in many temples one will find that chants, prayers and sermons are delivered in the language of the people.

Among the seven petitions listed above, three are self-explanatory, but four are of particular interest because they reflect some important doctrines. We will look at these four because they help us understand the meaning behind the action.

Petition one: 'the prostrations'

These differ according to various postures, from the simple to the more complicated. The first is putting the hands together in front of the chest and bowing slightly. This can be from a standing or fully prostrate position. Then in addition to the first position, the joined hands may be moved from high above the forehead, downwards to the lips and then the chest. This is to symbolise that mind, body and speech should engage together in the act of devotion. Often there will be full prostration three times, in remembrance of the Three Gems: the Buddha, the *Dharma*, and the Sangha.

Petition three (confession)

The following words may be used:

> The sin that has been done by me,
> Through despising mother and father,
> Through not understanding the Buddhas,
> And through not understanding the good.

> The sin of deed, word and thought
> The three fold wickedness that I have done
> All that will I confess
> Standing before the Buddhas.

This informs us that there is a comprehensive recognition of 'sin' or 'transgression' in terms of deed, word and thought. Although it is confessed, 'standing before the Buddhas', there is no indication of receiving forgiveness; naturally so, for the Buddha taught that we are already judged by our sin, rather than for it, and since the Buddha only exists now within the *Dharma*, there is nobody to forgive, in the sense that sin has been committed against God, or a god.

Petition six: the 'Bodhisattva vow'

Living beings are without number: I vow to row them to the other shore.

Defilements are without number: I vow to remove them from myself.

The teachings are immeasurable: I vow to study them and practise them.

The way is very long: I vow to arrive at the end.

This petition indicates that defilements can only be removed by 'vowing to remove them myself'.

Petition seven: the giving away of merit

This prayer is a protection against selfishness and reflects a 'vicarious' element to Buddhist petition:

My own self and my pleasures, my righteous past, present and future, may I sacrifice without regard, in order to achieve the welfare of all beings.

Other liturgies used in public worship will depend upon the particular culture, country and expression of Buddhism.

Worship at Home

Most heads of families (or whoever is responsible) rise very early in the morning and engage in a series of devotions which will include meditating on the *Dharma*, praying, and making offerings. There will be a shelf, recess or perhaps a room in which there will be a family shrine which will include at least one Buddhist image. The devotions are 'representative' in that whoever engages in them is doing so on behalf of the family. Special prayers and offerings by and for the family are made on special occasions, which may relate to the Buddha's life, or some special activity of the family, such as 'housewarming', praying for the sick, birth, or death. When a ceremony relates to death, Buddhist monks will be invited to the home to lead worship.

Pilgrimages along the Buddhist Trail

Since the *Dharma* teaches a way, an eightfold 'path', it is not surprising that early devotees would want to visit what would be perceived naturally to be holy places. There are many famous pilgrimage centres, especially those that relate to some important event in the life of the Buddha. Before he died, Gotama had indicated his approval of four important places that could be visited. With the demise of Buddhism in India, these places were abandoned. It was not until the late nineteenth century that pilgrimages were revived as a result of the Mahabodhi Society. Some important centres are as follows:

1. The Lumbini Park Grove

The birthplace of the Buddha. A famous monument was erected by Emperor Ashoka in the third century BC. This is situated in a very remote area of Northern India/ Southern Nepal and is still difficult to reach. So much more merit will be gained by the devotee who proceeds along this arduous journey. As recently as May 1996, *The Middle Way Journal* reports a discovery of a 'sacred stone' marking the exact birthplace of the Buddha. Although there have been disputes concerning this for the last 2,500 years, archaeologists from Nepal, India, Pakistan, Sri Lanka and Japan have now unearthed conclusive evidence. Relics were excavated from a chamber sixteen feet under the Mayadevi Temple in Lumpini, 200 miles south-west of Nepal's capital, Khatmandu. This find, say the archaeologists, proves without further doubt that this is where the Buddha was born. The stone marking the Buddha's birthplace was found on top of a layered brick platform dating back to the era of Emperor Asoka, who visited Lumpini nearly 400 years after Queen Maya walked from the sacred pond into the forest to deliver her son. Little wonder this has become the most desired place for pilgrimage.

2. Bodhi Gaya

This is the site of the Buddha's enlightenment and is therefore the most sacred of all pilgrimage sites. The present Bo tree is purported to be a descendant of the very tree under which the Buddha was enlightened. It has been claimed that visiting the place 'where it all happened' earns merit for a better reincarnation, and bestows blessings on the devotee. Adjacent to the tree is the Mahabodhi (Great Enlightenment) Temple. It dates from about the second century AD, but it is said that the foundations go back to a much earlier date. There are dozens of smaller buildings erected by various schools of Buddhism, all celebrating what to them is the most important event in history. Pilgrims walk around the tree, say prayers and offer flowers.

3. The Deer Park

This centre (near Benares) is famous because it is reported to be the place where the Buddha preached his first sermon. There is a massive statue of the Buddha in a very large temple called the Mulaganghakati sanctuary.

4. Kushinara

This centre, in Uttra Pradesh, is the site where the Buddha died. There are Burmese, Tibetan and Chinese monasteries and the ruins of many ancient stupas in the area. Devotees circumambulate three times round the stupas in the name of the Three Gems: the Buddha, the *Dharma* and the Sangha.

Apart from these 'international' centres of pilgrimage, each Buddhist country will have various special shrines, or centres of annual pilgrimage of their own. These will have been established for many different reasons. They could be special stupas in which it is rumoured, there are relics of the Buddha. For instance in Kandy, Sri Lanka, there is an important place of pilgrimage because it is claimed that one of the Buddha's teeth is there. Burma is reputed to have a relic of the Buddha's hair in the famous Shwe Dagon Pagoda in Yangon (Rangoon).

Examples of the Buddha's footprint are to be found all over Asia and some of them are reputed to have special powers. Adam's peak in Sri Lanka is most famous with pilgrims visiting from all over the world. This is nearly seven thousand feet high and a mark in the rock at the top is purported to be the Buddha's footprint. It may be added that this particular footprint is claimed by Portuguese Christians to have belonged to St Thomas while Hindus claim the footprint to be that of the god Shiva. Another important centre, the most famous outside India, is Borobodur in Java. This impressive range of Buddhist images set in circular and square terraces has vivid pictorial carvings in the walls depicting the Buddha's lives in animal and human forms.

The motives for pilgrimages can be varied. They may include almost trivial reasons, such as a desire to pass examinations, or more serious, such as the need for physical healing. It may be to gain more merit for the next life, or as a method of resolving some personal business, or family problem.

1. Jack Kornfield, *Living Buddhist Masters* (Unity Press, 1977), pp. 16–19.
2. Thomas Merton, *An Essay on Transcendent Experience*, R. M. Bucke Memorial Society, Vol. 1, No. 2, September 1966.
3. See Buddhist Scriptures (Penguin Classics, 1969), pp. 116–17 for this complicated analysis.
4. Ibid., p. 132.
5. *A Lion Handbook: The World's Religions* (Lion Publishing, 1982), p. 237.
6. Ann Bancroft, *Religions of the East* (Heinemann, 1974), p. 122.
7. Ibid., p. 76.
8. W. Owen Cole, *Six Religions of the Twentieth Century* (Hulton Educational, 1984), p. 151.

6

Ethics and Morality – Virtues and Vices

The Buddha's first sermon is said to have set in motion the eternal wheel of *Dharma*. At the hub of this wheel is the Eightfold Path, also referred to as the fourth Noble Truth; the discovery of which was the climax of the Buddha's enlightenment, the way of escape from his endless round of existences and release into Nirvana. There is no question that this teaching aims at guiding the devotee to the highest level of moral attainment. The emphasis on moral issues is without doubt the most detailed in any religion. The concept of a society regulated in accordance with the *Dharma* is an essential presupposition in all countries where Buddhism is predominant. No other belief system would require its leaders to take vows upon themselves in order to comply with 227 most fastidious regulations, such as those required for an ordained Buddhist monk.

Paradoxically, rather than expecting that this one set of rules would be required for everybody, a graduated scale is worked out, so that for those following at a lesser level (or perhaps one might say, from a distance), the expectations or requirements may be different. For instance, while sexual intercourse would be prohibited for a monk or nun, it would be regarded as normal for a lay person. All forms of alcohol would be forbidden at one level, but would be acceptable in moderation at another.

This desire for 'perfection' or wholeness does not focus on personal or social behaviour alone. For some schools, it extends to being concerned for the environment, so that there would be 'wholeness' and harmony within the individual, in the community and in nature. All of this can be achieved only by beginning and progressing along the Eightfold Path. Each of the eight listed categories of the path is prefixed with the word 'right'. This is not a good translation of the original which could be rendered more accurately 'highest' or 'perfect'. So these categories are no less than the highest and most perfect possible goals for a person to aim at personally, socially and environmentally.

Many elements of the Eightfold Path are directed towards suppression of the bad, and affirmation of the good in a person. They could be interpreted as a type of 'moral rearmament', a drawing upon inner resources of strength from the storehouse of one's own emotional, intellectual and volitional faculties. Christmas Humphries states:

> In spite of help which each may give to each, in the final stages of the Path, we walk alone. The Buddhist attitude is summed up in one of the most famous of its Scriptures, the Maha-ParinabbanaSutta. 'Therefore, O Ananda, take the Self as a lamp; take the Self as a refuge, Betake yourselves to no external refuge. Look not for refuge to anyone besides yourselves. Work out your own salvation with diligence.' No louder clarion call to self-reliance has ever been given than is contained in these few words.[1]

It is understood that however immoral or ethically corrupt a person may be, somewhere down in the depths of their being one will find a 'well of goodness'. The disclosure that this dormant essential goodness of the person, (the 'real you'?) really exists, is sometimes neglected by interpreters of Buddhist doctrine because at first sight, it may not be apparent. There is record of the Buddha taking the time to visit a notorious bandit, because he saw that only a brief exhortation would make him change his ways, become a monk and attain Nirvana. This inner purity called *Tathagata-garbha* is interpreted as 'the Buddha nature', which is understood to be 'resident' within every person. It may be hidden, obscure, buried, dormant, or whatever, but it *is* there and the consequence of adhering to the *Dharma* is to ensure that it 'slips anchor' and is allowed to float naturally to the surface of one's consciousness. Such teaching concerning a person's essential goodness is of course totally contrary to Christian teaching, which postulates that individuals are essentially sinful, contaminated and conditioned by this innate, oppressive power within, while at the same time, totally helpless and unable to marshal any inner resources to deal with it.

The Eightfold Path is divided into three areas each of which has a particular focus. They are:

The Eightfold Path	*Three foci*
1. Right views	
2. Right motives	= Wisdom (*prajya*)
3. Right speech	
4. Right conduct	= Morality (*sila*)
5. Right means of livelihood	
6. Right effort	
7. Right mind control	= Concentration (*samadhi*)
8. Right meditation or serenity	

The middle section of the foci above, numbers 3, 4 and 5, are concerned with right speech, right conduct and right livelihood which are called *sila* or 'highest moral perfections'. It is necessary to expand briefly on points 3 to 5 because they inform us with issues of morality and ethics.

Point 3: Right speech (samma waca)
This precept is regarded as the most important because lying or 'falsehood' would be the opposite of telling the truth. One passage in the *Dharma* indicates that if a person

has no sense of shame when intentionally lying, then that person is capable of any other misdeed. Any form of verbal deception must be avoided at all costs, because it not only destroys one's own integrity, but goes against the very idea of pursuing 'truth', which is the objective of Buddhism. This is explained in negative and positive terms. Negatively, 'right speech' means not engaging in gossip, not being negative towards another person or institution with the intention of destroying relationships; not engaging in idle chatter, bragging or using flattery; being free from dogmatic assertions or hypnotic suggestions. Positively, it means having the sensitivity to state what needs to be said at the appropriate time, always using kind speech, always choosing one's words carefully, always spreading harmony and using language which is gentle, comforting, and pleasing to the ear.

Point 4: Right action (Samma kammanta)

This is defined by the Buddha in his first sermon as 'abstaining from taking life, from taking what is not given, from carnal indulgence'. It is any action that emerges from a pure unhindered mind.

As usual, right action is defined in both negative and positive terms. Negatively it is expressed in 'the five precepts', *Pancha sila*. These are vows to abstain from killing, stealing, sensuality, lying and taking intoxicating liquor or drugs. Positively, right action is the avoidance of all that would detract from following the higher life and doing good. Many commentaries have been written, expanding the precise meaning of each word. For instance, 'abstain from taking life' has been interpreted in a conservative sense, that is not taking the life of a person i.e. murder; or more liberally it would extend to not taking the life of any good or bad creature from ant, poisonous snake, mosquito, to fish or animal. This could be further interpreted in terms of injuring or harming *any* living thing and even to harming anything inanimate thereby indicating ecological concern (see below on green issues).

'Abstaining from sexual misconduct' can also be

interpreted in a liberal or conservative fashion. What lies behind sexual behaviour? Is it control or suppression? This would be an important question for the devotee. In spite of the fact that the Buddha warned 'Of all the lusts and desires, there is none so powerful as sexual inclination,' sexual misconduct could be broadly interpreted by some to extend beyond what would be commonly held as the normal parameter of legitimate sexual behaviour within a family, to any sexual behaviour, gay, lesbian, or whatever, as long as mutual trust and respect existed between the partners. There are special weekend study courses and evening studies in Buddhism arranged for gay people at some Buddhist centres in this country, particularly the London Buddhist Centre at Covent Garden and Water Hall Suffolk. The advertisement for these courses does not question the moral correctness of homosexuality, it simply states that 'meditation and Buddhism can be practised by anyone irrespective of race, sex, sexuality or cultural background'.[2]

Point 5: Right (means of) livelihood (Samma ajiva)
While this prescribes the type of work one may or may not engage in, it has an extended meaning to cover 'lifestyle'. One commentator encouragingly states that if our daily work or employment enhances the search for and understanding of ourselves and the Dharma, then no matter how boring or futile it may appear to others, it could well be the job for us.

Using this criterion as a measure, it would be simple to say that any type of work that had questionable moral overtones should be avoided, for this would detract from pursuing the true path. Working for a brothel, in a gamblers' den, in a whisky factory would be unacceptable, or for example in an armaments factory, as true Buddhism holds to pacifism. What about working in a laboratory that engages in medical research where animals (all life is sacred?) are used for experiments? Should one be a representative for a company that produces chemicals that destroy insects? These are some of the ethical issues that a devout Buddhist is confronted with on a regular basis.

Green Issues

Right livelihood for many will extend to a rejection of any lifestyle that would contribute to the wanton destruction of our environment. So it is not only interpreted as engaging in types of remunerative employment that may destroy the environment, but all forms of everyday living. There will always be anomalies between what is taught and what is practised, there are Buddhist countries where forests are being denuded at an alarming rate. This to many Buddhists would be contrary to their own ethical persuasion.

There are very few Buddhist Scriptures that make direct reference regarding the environment, nevertheless general principles can be applied. For instance there is a story in the *Dhammapada Athatakha* (a commentary on the *Dhammapada*) which is interpreted in contemporary terms to environmental concerns in the world today:

When Samavati, the queen-consort of King Udena offered Ananda 500 garments, Ananda received them with great satisfaction. The king, hearing of it, suspected Ananda of dishonesty and asked what he would do with the garments. Ananda replied 'Many of the brothers are in rags. I am going to distribute the garments among them.' 'What will you do with the old garments?' 'We will make bed-covers out of them.' 'What will you do with the old bed-covers?' 'We will make pillowcases.' 'What will you do with the old pillowcases?' 'We will make floor-covers.' 'What will you do with the old floor covers?' 'We will make foot-towels out of them.' 'What will you do with the old foot towels?' 'We will use them for mops.' 'What will you do with the old mops?' 'Your Highness, we will tear them into pieces, mix them with mud and use the mud to plaster the house walls.'[3]

If ever there was an ingenious sensitive story which would

encourage the modern principle of recycling matter, it is this one.

While it may be true that there are no *direct* references to care of the environment, some enthusiasts believe many of the principles within the Eightfold Path may be applied to contemporary green issues. In the 1996 Summer issue of *Dharma Life* magazine, there is an article written by *Saramati* (Dr Alan Sponberg), where he advocates 'the greening of the *Dharma*' for today's followers of the Path. He realises that this 'greening' must have justification from the *Dharma* itself and interprets some of the *Dharma* passages as follows:

> Activism on behalf of the environment is, I believe, a suitable, even necessary form of Buddhist practice in today's world. But, Buddhist activism can ultimately be effective only to the extent that it is grounded in basic *Dharma*. So how are we to make the link? There are many passages in traditional Buddhist texts that express an appreciation of nature and counsel respect towards all life forms. Where though do we find advice about actively advocating an eco-centric concern for the environment? Where can we find guidance for mounting a demonstration (as did a group of FWBO Buddhists in the Northwest (US) at the site of the world's first plutonium reactor and the US's worst radioactive waste dump)? Where can we glean advice about living today in a manner that becomes increasingly sensitive to our fundamental, eco-centric inter-relatedness? We can begin by reflecting on one of the most basic formulations of Buddhist practice, the path of 'threefold learning'. This charts three steps toward an enhanced ethical sensibility: cultivation of skilful conduct, practice of meditation, and development of insight into the nature of existence ... Guidance in practising the threefold way is readily available in contemporary translations of Buddhist texts, and aspiring green Buddhists would do well to ground their practice within traditional approaches.

The article then seeks to apply the path of 'threefold learning' to a simple lifestyle; to do no harm to anything living, which would include both fauna and flora. Emerging from the practice of meditation there should be positive feelings of loving-kindness, sympathetic joy, compassion and equanimity. This is interpreted to mean for instance, that 'an ecologically minded Buddhist could take up the practice of generating "metta" or loving kindness, directing this toward himself, then towards a friend, towards a "neutral" person, an enemy . . . finally extend this to all beings.'

Whether such interpretation can or should really extend towards ecological issues, is of course a matter of interpretation. The writer of the article acknowledges that:

> Perhaps this is also why Buddhism historically has seen no need to develop a special separate position on nature and ecology. And indeed we might well be justified in concluding that Buddhism has no particular environmental ethic at all. By the same token, given that the *Dharma* cannot be practiced without completely transforming one's every response to the environment, we would also conclude that, by its very nature Buddhism *is* an environmental ethic.

But the concept of harmony, peace, respecting life in all its forms is surely quite a legitimate interpretation of Buddhist principles and practices even when it is extended to the environment.

It is interesting to note that Buddhists in Britain do interact with an expanding network of protest movements such as the so called 'Direct Action Movement' (the 'eco-warriors'), comprising all sorts of people who are disenchanted with government policies on various issues, especially road building, and transporting of animals out of the country. A writer poses the problem. 'The question of appropriate responses to perceived injustice has always been an issue within Buddhism. As it says in the *Dhammapada*; "hatred is never pacified by hatred in this world hatred is only pacified by love".' A network of 'Engaged Buddhists' visited the scene of protest surrounding the construction of the Newbury by-pass. They faced a dilemma because they could not reconcile their non violent philosophy with the violent nature of the protestations. One person said 'After Newbury, I felt that if it gets any worse than this I am pulling out of direct action movement. Pouring xxxx on a bailiff's head is not non-violence!'[4]

Other Rules or Precepts

While it has been noted that there are 227 regulations for the ordained monk, lay people (in most schools), may choose to follow either the five precepts, the eight precepts, or the ten precepts. Each set of precepts becomes more rigorous in its demands beyond the others, in terms of degrees of intensity or strictness. For the sake of clarity the groups are classified as follows: there are 'the lesser precepts' (five), 'the great precepts' (eight), and 'the greatest precepts' (ten).

There is a difference between the five precepts and the eight precepts in that the third rule of the fifth precept which states 'avoid unchaste sexual conduct' is changed to a more strict position in the eighth precept to state 'avoid all sexual activity'. The last three in the eight precepts which go beyond the first five, relate to abstaining from (sixth) eating at an unreasonable time; (seventh) dancing, singing, music and visiting shows, wearing garlands, perfumes or fine clothes; (eighth) sleeping on high beds i.e. not sleeping on the floor.

The ten precepts become even more confusing but are generally reserved for novices – apprentice monks, whose intention is to become ordained. They are intensified and extended. The previous precepts are increased by stages with such injunctions as vowing to abstain from handling gold or silver, and not to eat anything after midday.

Political Issues

It has been noted, that political and environmental issues are sometimes taken up enthusiastically by monks in the *Sangha* and by lay people. Monks have, at times, been at the forefront of political protest when they have felt that their very existence or the future of Buddhism is being threatened. Such protest is in progress, particularly in Tibet and Burma (Myanmar). There are continuing efforts to negotiate with political forces, so that a person may be a loyal citizen within any particular political ideology while at the same time maintaining his Buddhist beliefs. This has proved impossible in certain places especially for Buddhists in Burma who attempted a synthesis between Buddhism and Marxist social theory, without success. They are now trying to live under a military dictatorship, equally with no success. People like Au Sang Su Ching, Burmese Nobel Peace Prize winner, a staunch advocate of a peaceful political process based on Buddhist ethics, are honoured and respected as examples of this approach.

There have also been reports regarding a famous Vietnamese Zen monk Thich Nhat Hahn, now living in France, who has vainly attempted to find a Buddhist answer to the ongoing problem of military conflict in his country.[5] These figures have triggered a growing interest in attempts to find a 'middle path' between Western Capitalism and Marxism and the concept of pacifistic 'people power'. In response to the incoherent position that Buddhists hold with regard to modern economic and political ideologies, there has been increasing pressure to organise an international body to discuss these issues. In spite of some international gatherings there have been so many differences regarding the 'official position' on various issues, such as human rights, international disarmament, injustice, that there have been few positive results in addressing these problems.

Nevertheless, being aware of fellow Buddhists' dilemmas in restricted countries, like Burma, devotees in democratic lands have been trying to interpret Nationalism, Socialism, and other ideologies in order that they may be able to exist together harmoniously. One particular group in Japan calling themselves the *Niponzan Myohoji*, in response to the atom bomb and all other forms of war and violence, have set up 'peace pagodas' in many countries round the world. In 1973 one was built in Milton Keynes and then on the 31 May 1986 a ceremony and celebrations were held for the first anniversary of the London Peace Pagoda in Battersea Park. Bishop Trevor Huddleston presided over the events as Chairman of the Friends of the London Peace Pagoda.

Ethical Issues Regarding the Sick, Society and the Family

There are particular philosophical or doctrinal tensions with regard to the physically handicapped and those who have contracted some form of serious disease such as AIDS or leprosy. While the concept of the Bodhisattva portrays compassion for those who are sick or under-privileged, and the Buddha himself stated 'whoever wishes to take care of me should take care of the sick', there remains ambiguity centred on the concept of karma. If the law of karma delivers the just deserts of evil committed in a previous existence, then people with leprosy would be receiving the just rewards of this inviolable law of cause and effect. To show compassion for, or give assistance to such a sick person, is to attempt to reverse, mitigate against, or alleviate that which karma has already determined, or predetermined as a just judgment for previous evils committed.

Social ethics
In spite of such anomalies or contradictions, humanitarian relief is effectively carried out with compassion by Buddhist devotees of every school. Social activism has increasingly been emphasised in most schools, involving monks in education, social concerns, such as using Temples for

assisting people who have contracted AIDS or need to be helped in terms of drug addiction. Because this has been the specialist activity of just one or two temples, it is regarded by many as mere 'tokenism', touching the tip of the iceberg, and therefore relatively insignificant in terms of restraining the ever growing influences of declining morality and escalating modernity. But the question as to whether Buddhism, the monks and the laity together, can adequately address problems of growing secularisation, over-population, prostitution, political and religious corruption, and economic exploitation remains unanswered. Can Buddhism retain its identity, respond effectively and survive in the midst of these twentieth-century problems?

There can be no greater struggle for the survival of Buddhism today, than in Tibet, where the conflict of interest between the exiled Dalai Lama and the Chinese Government, who have been accusing him of forging Buddhist texts, altering the teachings and violating the principles of the *Dharma*, continues unabated. They say, Buddhism clearly advocates detachment (*Upekka*) and disinterest in all worldly affairs of state, especially political affairs that call for democracy or independence.

Continuing with the theme of social ethics, the extent to which the concept of 'compassion' is extended to every living creature can be seen by the establishing of such organisations as The International Buddhist Relief Organisation, which has been set up in Birmingham to 'relieve suffering of people everywhere regardless of their status, creed, or geographical location, who are in hardship or distress as a result of local or national disaster or as a result of their social or economic circumstances in accordance with Buddhist doctrine and principles and to extend such help also to animals everywhere who are in need of care and attention'.

Animal welfare is therefore an intrinsic part of Buddhist ideology. But there comes a problem if and when an animal should be put out of its misery. While the whole aim of Buddhism is to alleviate suffering, the concept of taking life in any or all its forms, even to alleviate suffering, is nevertheless wrong. 'Killing it would be seen as not much different from killing a human,' for animals and humans are essentially the same. This of course would appear to be quite logical, since animals in this life may actually have been humans who have gone back down the scale of reincarnations because of bad karma, or on the other hand, the animal may be waiting for the next life, to be reborn up the scale to become human because as an animal it has acquired good karma. This of course raises another philosophical question – if karma is predetermined on the basis of good and bad (which it is), then that presupposes one must have a conscience which *knows* good and bad and also a will that deliberately *chooses* either good or bad. How far can one extend these faculties of conscience and will down the animal line in terms of being capable of making *moral* choices? If the faculty of moral choice does not extend to an ant, or microbe or whatever, then through this inability it will be impossible for such creatures to attain a higher reincarnation. There appears to be a mystery as to how a scale is worked out to determine these matters.

As an illustration, a further dilemma would be, what does one do, if a dog contracts rabies? Would it be wrong to put down poisoned meat to kill off non-domesticated dogs that roam wild around some temples, which carry this deadly disease? How far down the line does one go in not taking life? What about mosquitoes? What about preventative medicine against germs? These after all are forms of life. Many would feel that these are areas to which the appropriate Buddhist word would be *avija* – we do not know.

Family

Compassion extends to social relationships within the family and community especially for the aged, those who are dying, and even to those who are 'the living dead' – those who have recently died, but are regarded as still living in the house.

Particular care is taken for those who are dying, so that

by assisting and comforting, the relatives will be helping the person to 'have a good death'. This is all in order 'that the best possible rebirth is obtained, within the limits set by previous karma.' There is an underlying assumption, that if things are done in the most careful and auspicious way, then merit may be transferred to the one passing over to the other side, thus adding to the weight of karmic force and enabling a better rebirth. Each school will have variations of emphasis, but all take very seriously the importance of 'sending off' the dead person is such a way that they are helped. Eastern Buddhism encourages the dying person to hold on to strings attached to a painting of *Amitabha*, symbolising being pulled along to the 'Pure Land' ahead. Prayers are made to the heavenly Bodhisattvas, appealing to them to transfer merit to the departing one. Tibetan Buddhism has a ceremony in which the *Tibetan Book of the Dead* is read, so that the person may be guided during the forty-nine day 'incubation' period which will determine what the next incarnation will produce, and help the person to be released from any lingering attachment they may have to their body, or their family.

Popular Folk Buddhists hold to many non-orthodox beliefs about the dead, which are very real to them. Many schools will have post-death ceremonies at various intervals, some ten days after death, some one hundred days. This is for two main reasons. First, to ensure the departed really has departed; second, if it is ascertained that the 'departed' has not yet departed, then to usher them along as speedily as possible on their journey – hoping against hope that they will be satisfied with the send-off and not stay around any longer. It is strange how often good, gracious, kind, benevolent people in their life-time can suddenly turn into crotchety, capricious, bad-tempered, malevolent 'spirits of the departed'. They are perceived to be waiting for the least pretext, the earliest opportunity, to get their own back and pounce on the living relatives, causing tragedy, illness or some other calamity. This is especially so if upon their demise they are not taken notice of, humoured, honoured and fed regularly. So it is no wonder that these sending-off ceremonies are conducted with such care on the one hand and enthusiasm on the other.

Other ethical values that are admirable are the sense of honour and respect given by younger people to the older in general and to parents in particular. This is especially so in the relationship between teacher and pupil and between religious teacher and disciple.

Western attitudes have spoiled all of this in many universities and colleges in Asia, where teenage subcultures, fed by antisocial anti-authoritarian values through the power of the media and music, have eroded the social structures and cohesiveness of many societies.

In Theravada Buddhism all young boys will spend at least one rainy season in a Buddhist temple, learning the elementary principles and practices of their faith. This is in order to gain merit for their parents. They use a lovely expression: 'Once supported by them I will now be their support; I will perform duties incumbent on them, keep up the lineage and tradition of my family make myself worthy of my heritage, and give alms on their behalf when they are dead.'[6]

In the code of discipline the *vinaya* Buddha is reported to have met a certain Sigala, who was worshipping in 'six directions' according to his father's dying wish. In order to make this ritual more socially meaningful, the Buddha instructed that, rather than just worshipping in six directions geographically which would be merely outward gestures, he should invest these 'six directions' with inner meaning. He should have proper reactions or responses towards six categories of people so as to maintain good relationships and harmony with them. So ingeniously the Buddha proposed that Sigala should have a right relationship to his parents (face east), to his teachers (face south), to his wife (face west) and to his friends (face north); he then added two unthought of directions – to servants and employees (face downwards) and to monks and other religious leaders (face upwards).

The roles of husband and wife in a family are particularly interesting – the problem is that different schools attribute different values to this relationship. Cultural values sometimes override religious ones, so in some countries women are regarded merely as property owned by men, to be used at will. In these cases there is little real inter-communication or warm relationship between the genders – women are made to feel as if they are on a lower level of existence than men. Men meet and interact with men, women socialise with women. There are promises that if a couple live harmoniously in this life, they may be reincarnated together in the next. The role of the wife and mother is vital in some countries, for she often holds the purse strings and is mainly responsible for the welfare of the children. Sadly, men often distance themselves from such mundane activities, sometimes with the excuse that they have work to do, as if the mother had no work. In fact she would normally have both the work at home and in the fields. The Zen emphasis is total equality between male and female, for both are seen as possessing the Buddha nature.

However, it is true to say that for most schools, females are regarded as not able to attain to Buddhahood until they have become male in the next reincarnation.[7] Their suffering is perceived as too great, in that they have to experience pain in childbirth and menstruation. In spite of this fundamental biological disadvantage, females are given a respected place in most schools of thought. They may assume leadership roles in community and government. They are accepted as teachers and trainers in the secular and lay world. They may give up all worldly ambition and become nuns.

Conclusion

Sages of the past have debated whether Buddhists have as the goal of their merit making, their own well being, or the benefit of another person. After all is it not the very essence of selfishness to pursue one's own salvation at all costs, regardless of anyone else? I recall an incident while having coffee in a certain country. A well-rounded healthy looking man approached the front of the shop with a rather large begging bowl asking for alms. Whereupon the owner immediately placed a generous offering in the bowl; and then looking at me asked 'Aren't you going to give anything?' I rejoined – 'Why did *you* give that man the money, did he need it?' 'No' was the reply, 'but I needed the merit I gained, by giving it to him.' Ethically, donating the money contributed in helping a perfectly healthy man along the path of laziness. Motivationally, it gave the shop owner the merit he wanted . . . or did it? For karma would surely determine that his motivation was wrong in the first place. But does karma then have 'cognisance' to be able to determine the motivation of that person? If karma has enough intelligence not to grant merit because of wrong motivation, then it can not be just an 'impersonal force' because impersonal force, while it may have power (like electricity), is not intelligent. Where does karma get its 'prescience' from? If on the other hand karma did grant merit although the motivation was wrong, then the whole principle of karma falls apart, for we discover that it is neither just nor reliable.

It does appear then, that there are two possible motivations, or 'driving forces' which pressurise people to attempt to conform or at least aim at the moral perfections of the Eightfold Path. They are both positive and negative. Positively, there is the belief that the all important merit will be accumulated (credited to one's spiritual bank account) by aiming at the highest perfection resulting in a higher life next time round. This conviction would be a most powerful driving force.

Conversely, if while knowing what one *should* be doing, what Path one *should* be following, one makes a series of wrong choices and indulges in behaviour that is known to be contrary to the right Pathway, indicating a *laisser faire*, 'couldn't care less' approach, then the fearful inviolable law of karma will kick into effect and determine that one's future reincarnation must inevitably be worse than one's present. For whatever we sow, that we must reap. One of the most famous statements of Christmas Humphries affirms this 'We are judged by our sins, not for them.' It is interesting from an ethical point of view that in his talk on 'Equanimity' at the Founders Day of The Buddhist Society on 13 April 1996, the Venerable B. Seelawimala stated 'If one wants to use the word punish, it is better to talk about our being punished *by* our misdemeanours, rather than *for* them. I believe that Christmas Humphries, when acting in his capacity as a judge, used to tell a convicted criminal that it was he the criminal who sent himself to prison as a result of his own actions. He said "Man is punished by his sins, not for them".' This interesting analogy does raise questions – to implement law, there must be a person (Christmas Humphries in this case), who is intelligent enough to give a sentence commensurate with the crime. So while in one sense the criminal is sent to prison because of his so-called misdemeanours, this is not the whole story – he is sent by Christmas Humphries also. To replace an intelligent person with some indeterminate impersonal force called karma, does not 'do justice' to the situation at all.

Having said this, the more thoughtful, philosophical or 'ideological' Buddhist interpretation would suggest, that if the reasons individuals propel themselves to achieve these goals are self-centred (accruing spiritual credit in one's own spiritual bank account), then even the achievement of moral purity in this life will be negated and not help in the next life because of wrong motivation.

Here we could find ourselves in a no-win situation. To 'desire' to attain is wrong we are taught, because all forms of desire are the root cause of suffering, yet on the other hand, to be totally detached and not to desire to attain is also wrong. Where does one go from here? Some may well ask, where is the middle way? Answers may be proffered but only in terms of 'antinomies' – contradictions between two logical conclusions. Now if that sounds 'un-reasonable', then do not worry. It is 'unreasonable'.

Because such 'truths' cannot be grasped by our normal reasoning faculties, there needs to be, we are told, an 'enlightening' process that transcends reasonableness, for things to become clear.

From a Christian point of view, this awesome determinative force of karma, this fear of being predestined in the future, on the basis of reliance on one's own pure motivation and unmitigated self-effort (non-effort?), in the present, can hold no attraction at all. The Bodhisattva concept, that there is One who sacrificially and willingly waits to help those who call upon him (Jesus Christ in this case), is really, in view of the rather dismal alternative prospect of self-attainment and effort, the good news one would desperately want to 'grasp' hold of. I recall once driving in a taxi in the middle of the hot season in Bangkok, where the atmosphere was so thick with car fumes, so heavy that one could hardly breathe; after being in a traffic jam for what seemed an eternity, the cab driver suddenly burst out 'Oh, if only this was my last life to live,' I responded by saying 'But surely you have not gained sufficient merit for that have you?' to which he replied 'Do you think I would be driving this thing down here, if I could be up there, of course I don't have enough merit.' I then asked 'If there was someone, who was good enough, and great enough who would be willing to transfer sufficient merit to you, so that you might be "delivered", what would you say to such an offer.' He replied simply 'That would be good news.'

The Christian response to this would mean that the Damocles sword of karma hanging above one would never be able to take its vengeance, the endless wheel would have come to a standstill, the sinner would neither be punished by nor for sins, for if the penalty has already been paid once for misdemeanour even, if it was paid for by a substitute, then the law disallows that it can be paid twice.

1. Christmas Humphries, *Buddhism* (Penguin Books, 1951), p. 95.

2. Brochure advertising Autumn/Spring meditation courses of the London Buddhist Centre FWBO.

3. See Summer issue of *Dharma Life* journal 1966.

4. FWBO Summer issue 1966, p. 26.

5. His last book *Living Buddha, Living Christ* (Putnam & Sons, 1995) is an over ambitious attempt to merge Buddha and Christ resulting as one reviewer put it, 'In World view confusion – an interpretative error that reads a text according to a perspective that is alien to the text itself.' This book says the reviewer (Douglas Groothius) is one of those attempts to 'defend the indefensible', i.e. that Christ and the Buddha are the same.

6. Peter Harvey, *An Introduction to Buddhism* (Cambridge University Press, 1990), p. 213.

7. Ibid., p. 216.

7

Leadership Structures and Religious Offices

Taking Refuge

Initiation as a monk into the official Buddhist order requires that all prospective candidates repeat three times a particular formula which relates to 'The Three Gems': the Buddha, the *Dharma* and the Sangha. It is as follows:

To the Buddha I go for refuge.
To the *Dharma* (teaching) I go for refuge.
To the Sangha (order of monks) I go for refuge.

It is understood that taking refuge in the Buddha does not guarantee that the Buddha himself will extend 'salvation' to anyone, for the Buddha is not perceived as a Saviour figure – on the contrary he states 'Surely by oneself is evil done, by oneself one becomes impure, by oneself evil is avoided, by oneself one becomes pure. Purity and impurity are individual. No one purifies another.' Nor is 'taking refuge in the *Dharma*' understood to mean that the *Dharma* of itself is efficacious or redemptive – it merely points the way to liberation from the four aspects of *dukkha* (suffering) which govern existence namely: 1. *Dukkha sacca* – the nature of imperfect existence. 2. *Dukkha satya* – the nature of *causation* affecting imperfect existence. 3. *Dukkha Norodhasacca/satya* – the removal or disappearance of imperfect existence and the realisation of freedom in perfect existence to Nirvana. 4. *Dukka magga/marga satya* – the way to knowledge and experience of the supreme life.

It has been suggested that the translation of the words 'take refuge' is misleading because of its broader meaning in English than the original, which could have been translated 'guide' – so that the recitation would be 'to the Buddha I go as my guide, to the *Dharma* I go as my guide, to the Sangha I go as my guide'. Taking refuge in the Sangha presupposes passing through an official ordination ceremony where, having repeated the above Three Gems formula the ordinand is then required to promise in the original Pali language: 'From this day forth I undertake' and he will then chant ten commandments which he vows to keep. They are listed below:

1. To abstain from destroying all forms of life.
2. To abstain from taking what is not given to me . . . (to not steal).
3. To abstain from sexually immoral conduct.
4. To abstain from false speech.
5. To abstain from intoxicating liquor.
6. To abstain from eating at the wrong hour (after midday).
7. To abstain from dancing, singing with instruments, shows, fairs (amusements).
8. To abstain from decoration, perfumes, garlands.
9. To abstain from sleeping in high, large or comfortable beds.
10. To abstain from accepting gold, silver (money).

The ordination ceremony is both detailed and complicated. At one stage during the proceedings the ordinand will be handed his begging bowl and robes. He will be publicly interviewed by the officiant, the President or Abbot of the temple, who will expect responses from the ordinand to the following questions:

'Have you any such diseases as these; Leprosy?' 'No, Lord.' 'Boils?' 'No Lord.' 'Itch?' 'No Lord.' 'Asthma?'

'No Lord.' 'Epilepsy?' 'No Lord.' 'Are you a human being?' 'Yes Lord.' 'Are you male?' 'Yes Lord.' 'Are you free from debt?' 'Yes Lord.' 'Are your alms bowl and robes complete?' 'Yes Lord.' 'What is your name?' 'Lord I am called . . .'

Following these responses the Abbot will preach a short sermon which includes solemn warnings for not keeping the commandments, and following this, the ceremony ends. While there will be different styles of ordination ceremonies and rituals according to the differing schools of Buddhism in different countries, there are nevertheless some common elements throughout Theravada Buddhism and to a lesser degree in Mahayana Buddhism.

In all cases, the ordination results in incorporation into the Sangha, the monastic order, which is understood as the community of monks past, present and future. It can be interpreted broadly as the fellowship of all those who have followed in the footsteps of the Buddha. In actual practice there is a narrower definition, for only the Sangha includes those celibates who have abandoned normal family life to join the monastic family; those who are willing to subscribe to the 227 particular laws and regulations of the order (the *Mahavibhanga*) which are chanted (rehearsed) twice each month on the waxing and waning of the moon; those who are totally committed to worship and work together to maintain and promote the Buddhist cause.

Organisationally the Sangha is the administrative structure into which the monk is ordained. In most countries it will normally be a pyramid type structure (closely resembling government structures), with a council of ecclesiastical ministers, normally operating from a capital city, who govern and control by passing directives down to abbots in charge of local temples. The head of the Sangha will be the Supreme Patriarch who is chosen on the basis of rank, charisma and influence. There will be an annual assembly and presidents and vice presidents of the council will be chosen from the assembly. This council will elect a judiciary which will be responsible for dealing with breaches of discipline which occur quite regularly.

The emphasis of the Sangha is generally speaking non-political, and concentrates on maintaining discipline, devotions, merit making, meditation and study. In different countries there may be special Buddhist schools comparable to church schools in England, and also universities which are established to reinforce Buddhist morals and teaching.

Temple Life

For the most part Buddhist activities will centre on the temple and its environs; although there are some orders of mendicant monks who roam the land with 'no fixed abode', they will ensconce themselves in local temples and take part in their proceedings during the rainy season.

Most villages will have at least one temple and in the towns there may be dozens. There will usually be the main building or preaching hall for worship (*Vihara*). Almost all temples will have a *stupa* within the compound. This is a type of monument in which there may be buried relics or remains (*mahataat*) of the Buddha. The stupas had pre-Buddhist antecedents and functionally were the same as sepulchres; they were used as burial mounds to inter important warriors or kings. As the style of Buddhist images changed according to art forms and cultures down the ages, so the design of stupas varies in different lands and cultures.

There will generally be a number of buildings within the temple grounds. These include the Sangha 'bote' where the council meets. Also there will almost always be a sacred Bo tree in the temple surrounds, planted in remembrance of the place where the Buddha was enlightened. There will also be numerous other pavilions or *salas*, used for all sorts of social and religious activities.

In many countries, all buildings face the rising sun in deference to the fact that the Buddha was facing East when he was enlightened. The main edifice will generally be incredibly ornate, with thousands upon thousands of small pieces of coloured mirror glass embedded into the walls. These will reflect the sun in the mornings, thus making the whole building appear to glow with radiance. Inside the main temple, the walls and ceilings will be decorated with beautiful depictions of the life of the Buddha taken from the *Jataka* legends. There are no chairs, pews or furnishings except an ornate altar/chair/throne reserved for the teaching monk which will be used when expounding the *Dharma*. At the Western end of the temple there will be numerous Buddhist images, in various postures reflecting either the era when they were cast, or some particular event in the life of the Buddha. These will be embellished with incense sticks and candles. It is here in front of the massive images that the devout, having taken off their shoes at the entrance, will prostrate themselves or kneel; then they will light incense sticks and make petitions and offerings. They will sometimes purchase very expensive gold leaf and apply this to the images while praying and making obeisance. The temple surrounds, kept clean by the novices, are used for all social activities of the community as well as daily worship and special worship on holy days.

At day-break, following morning prayers at 5.30 a.m. when the monks will confess their sins, they gather together with a number of young temple boys (novices) and will then proceed bare footed out of the temple in a single line. They will collect food from outside the houses of the faithful devotees who will be waiting at the roadside to give their offerings. A short prayer will sometimes be muttered by the monk and the devotees will go home happy that by this good deed, they will have gained more merit for their future reincarnation. Normally it will be a female member of the family who will make the offerings.

The Buddhist monk will never say 'thank you' because the act of receiving the food enables the devotee to gain merit. The monk will show no appreciation, for it is his duty to practise detachment or indifference in all situations. It would be quite possible for a mother to bow down and offer obeisance to her own son, perhaps one of the novices who is begging. The mother would be acknowledging in her own son a representation of the Buddha himself. This is seen as giving the Buddha honour, symbolised by the saffron robe the son is wearing.

If a monk breaks one of the regulations, lay people will speak of such a monk as 'offending the saffron robe'. This is regarded as an expression of offence to the Buddha, or the *Dharma*. Monks are forbidden (just one of the two hundred and twenty seven regulations) to cast their eyes either upwards or more than two metres beyond themselves while in procession for their daily food, so that they will not be tempted by some of the pretty ladies who will be making their offerings. Monks are generally not expected to engage in any form of 'secular' work, including farming, trading, or business. However, there are exceptions in some schools. A large number of monasteries in Sri Lanka do engage in commercial activities in order to maintain themselves and the community of the faithful. In China too, some have acted as 'pawnbrokers' or 'money lenders' for the community and previously have run large markets. Rinzai Zen temples in Japan at one time ran fleets of trading ships to China. In pre-Communist Tibet the monasteries were key economic institutions and engaged in arranging loans and investments. These activities spread across Theravada, Mahayana and Zen Buddhism.

Normally monks are not allowed to support themselves with their own funds because they are not allowed to handle gold or silver. Property cannot be owned by a monk, nor should they be involved in any political process or party. However, as has been witnessed in Myanmar (Burma), Sri Lanka, Vietnam and Tibet, monks can be a substantial political force in fighting for freedom and resisting detrimental change to their cultures by external or internal forces.

Monks are forbidden to attend all sporting events including football games and any communal social activities that would come under the category of 'amusement'; this would be on pain of expulsion from the order if they infringe these regulations. These particular rules are especially difficult to keep since most of the communities' social life, including annual fun fairs, is centred on the temple. The annual fair will include all forms of entertainment, from dancing to boxing, to merry-go-rounds or anything else that will amuse the public. Sometimes one may observe monks peering wistfully from their tiny retreat houses, trying to appear quite detached and certainly not giving the impression that they are either watching or enjoying such events. Monks are invited on special occasions to dine at devotees' homes – especially to bless weddings and lead funeral ceremonies.

If a monk wishes to leave the Sangha, he simply pronounces the statement 'I hereby take leave of the Sangha, may you all remember me as a layman.' There are four rules, (three are taken from the ten ordination commandments) which if broken would demand immediate expulsion from the Sangha. They are:

1. If a monk should have sexual intercourse with anyone, the monk would no longer deserve to live in the community.
2. If a monk, whether he dwells in a village or in solitude, should take anything not given, he should no longer live in the community.
3. If a monk should intentionally take the life of a human being with his own hand or with a knife, or have a person assassinated, he has fallen into an offence which demands expulsion.
4. If a monk vainly with excessive self deceit and without basis of fact falsely claims to have realised and perceived superhuman states, or the fullness of enlightenment, he deserves expulsion.

A further thirteen offences – which would bring about suspension rather than expulsion – are chanted at least every fortnight to ensure the monks do not forget or transgress. Many of these offences centre on sexual temptation or deviation and go into considerable detail about what is not allowed for a monk.[1]

On a normal day, following breakfast the monks will assemble in the temple to chant the morning service in the Pali language, which none of the lay people who attend will understand. But this does not matter as long as the sound is audible, as merely the fact of coming within the earshot of the chants has of itself merit making value; it is therefore not regarded as a waste of time. While the main 'service' is going on, there may be other younger novices who would be reciting individually or together various selected rhythmic chants from parts of the Pali Scriptures.

Before noon, the monks will eat their last meal for the day and in the afternoon they will engage in further study, prayer or conversation. Morning and evening worship styles will vary according to the time of the year or lunar month in the Buddhist calendar. There are prescribed chants (comparable to collects in the Church of England) for the monks, sometimes intoned by the leader and sometimes chanted in unison.

The day to day routine of temple life is interrupted from time to time with numerous seasonal festivals and celebrations. The whole community will come together to enjoy a fairground type of atmosphere where dancing, boxing, fairs, floats and other processions are held. These celebrations generally are held at a particular time of the year, which will generally relate to some important aspect of the Buddha's life or teaching. One such occasion is the 'invoking of rain' ceremony at the beginning of the rainy season. A prayer for rain goes as follows: 'The Lord Buddha is omniscient; the precious *Dharma* is the highest thing in the world, the holy Sangha consist of those established in the way and the Fruit. These are the Three Gems. By virtue of the power of the Three Gems may rain fall in due season. May good fortune come to us all.'

Of particular importance are those occasions where novices are ordained to become monks, and are presented with their saffron robes, or when there are National Buddhist holidays. During these times the monks are specially blessed with offerings of tobacco, incense, flowers, wash basins and other needful things. Strictly speaking a monk's material possessions should be just enough to carry around single handed. This would comprise clothing, an upper, lower and over robe, a belt, a bowl, a razor, a needle, a water strainer, a staff and a tooth pick. Also included may be sandals, a towel, extra work robes, a shoulder bag, an umbrella, books, writing materials, a clock and a picture of the monk's particular teacher.

The Scholastic Life

A major part of a monk's life is engaging in study and meditation. These can be divided into communal and individual activities. The study centres on observing and memorising in the original languages, large sections of the *Dharma* and the monastic code. Sometimes monks will specialise in one of these areas and thereby gain a reputation for either possessing 'knowledge' called 'book duty' or gaining spirituality, called 'insight duty', achieved through intensive meditation. Theravadin monks study the basic doctrines (*Vinaya*) plus the more interesting legends from the *Jataka* for use in sermons. They will also be required to memorise hundreds of the basic chants in the Pali language. Monks in China and Tibet will study the Chinese Canon which is also used in Korea, Vietnam and Japan (as indicated in Chapter 4). It is not widely acknowledged, but is nevertheless a fact, that the world's oldest books were printed using wooden blocks, a technique invented in AD 86 by the Chinese, in order to reproduce Buddhist chants.

In Tibetan Buddhism most of the Scriptures are inscribed on collections of oblong strips (about three inches wide and twelve inches long) of palm leaf or parchment. Monks may spend as much as five years in memorisation and study and some would then move on to a further seven years in a Tantric college in order to discover the secrets of the mystical Tantric texts. It is possible to study for twenty-five years in order to gain a 'Doctor of Buddhology' degree. There is high regard for scholarship in Buddhism and from time to time certain monks can gain a tremendous following, often through their charismatic preaching of some lesser known doctrine which may have been over-looked but then suddenly gains an enthusiastic acceptance because it appears to be new. Such preachers are often regarded as radical reformers within their particular schools. A book has been written specifically about such exponents, appropriately entitled *Living Buddhist Masters*.[2] In it Jack Kornfield lists at least fourteen famous contemporary scholars, renowned because of their way of life and their teaching.

The Meditative Life

Hundreds of meditation manuals have been produced by the different schools, all proffering helpful instructions on 'how to do it'. Someone has said that the art of meditation is comparable with learning to play a musical instrument. There are no short cuts in learning how to tune and play the mind, so that the effect will be truly harmonious rather than just a noise. Someone else has likened meditation to gardening; one cannot force plants to grow but one can provide them with the right conditions in order for them to grow and develop naturally. Yet another person compares the results of this penetrative meditation with the composition of a chorus or melody. The following quotation may sound complicated, but it is important because it seeks to explain the deeper meaning of meditation:

> No single sound or chord possesses duration and emotional value, but the continuous succession of sounds produces the phenomenon of a melody. And as a dissonance in the melody does not necessarily mean the end of the music, so the death of a being does not

necessarily mean the end of the chain of Conditional Dharmas. In most cases the Nexus of Conditioned Origination will continue after the person's death. Death itself is only a dharma of the chain – just as dissonance is an element of the melody . . . the very moment one becomes aware of separate tones, the enchantment collapses. In a similar way people are impressed by the world only as long as they regard it as something essential. When one day they see through themselves and the empirical world as phenomena produced by Conditioned dharmas, it dawns on them that from time immemorial they have been frightened by something illusory. It is this realisation which leads from knowledge to wisdom.[3]

In all schools, it is agreed that achieving a state of 'enlightenment' is the ultimate goal. The penultimate stage through meditation is the gaining of *pannya* or *prajna*, which means 'wisdom'. Such wisdom takes the mind deeper than mere study, even beyond acquiring 'knowledge' (*Jnanya*) of the unseen and the unknown. It constitutes a mind which is full of 'concentrated experiential wisdom' – this leads one further than all rational limitations, to a state of *sarvajnata* which means 'omniscience' – knowing all there is to know. But this does raise questions concerning the 'state of mind' of the devotee and there is some ambiguity in the way one interprets exactly what is happening to the mind when one has reached such a state.

Although some have translated the word *sati* as 'mind-*fullness*' the paradox is that the goal of meditation is neither mind-*fullness* and certainly not mind-*lessness*, but 'mind-*emptiness*'. For according to the teaching, it is only as one first attains the state of true emptiness that the mind can then progress to *sati* (awareness) which then leads on to a type of mind-fullness which has one particular sharp focus (concentration) and nothing else. This will then lead to a trance-like state – an 'altered state of consciousness' which can include mind-reading, the use of psychic powers, supposed memory recall of previous lives and clairvoyance and 'omniscience'.[4]

Into this recipe of ingredients that contribute to actualising the goal of meditation, one must add another extremely important constituent called *Upekka*. This means 'complete *evenness* of mind', or 'equanimity'. It is a balanced state of mind, free from both attachment and aversion, a state of neutrality, rooted in insight, it is equanimity amidst all the vicissitudes of life, of which there are eight; fame and ill-fame, praise and blame, gain and loss, happiness and unhappiness. In other words it is not wanting to want! It is that state of *jit wang* which simply means emptiness of mind. It is only when one is empty of all that attaches one to this world, that one can be filled with all that would bring release to the next world. At the risk of using a play on words, one must ask, does 'not wanting' mean having a *desire* to 'not want'? Then technically speaking it is wrong, so in the final analysis, must reach a stage of 'not wanting to want'. But let us look at some of the obstacles that stop most people from not wanting to achieve this state.

To attain to the state of total detachment, a condition where desire has been destroyed, one must overcome the following five hindrances:

1. *Sensual desire*: This is when the mind is diverted from the particular object of concentration, to something which might be more attractive for the moment. When this happens, the long process of meditation has to start all over again.
2. *Ill will*: This does not relate to a breakdown of relationships with other people, but a negative unwillingness to pursue the path ahead. The opposite to the concept of abandonment.
3. *Laziness, lethargy, drowsiness*: This is related to number two, but is a further step away from the goal in view, produced rather by a lack of motivation than just ill will.
4. *Anxiety, restlessness, worry*: All of this is produced

because of a feeling that one is not getting anywhere with the exercise at hand. Anxiety cripples the process of attainment.

5. *Double mindedness*: A mind that vacillates and wavers, feeling that the end in view is not worth the energy expended.

The particular 'tools' to aid concentration while meditating may vary according to a teacher's advice and the devotee's degree of detachment. The tool could be 'abstract' – a particular grace or virtue to emulate, or it could be 'concrete' in the sense of an object which has material substance – a flower or a landscape. For someone who may be continually tempted by lust, for instance, focusing on the thirty-two parts of the body (which would include all the unattractive parts, such as entrails, perspiration, mucus and excreta), would be a sure way of distracting someone with such a preoccupation! For others a very popular subject to concentrate on has been 'loving kindness' or *metta*. The preliminary focus would be on metta directed to oneself, in spite of one's faults and failings, then to focus metta on others in spite of their faults and failings. A further method is to focus intently on somebody who is greatly respected by the devotee. The aim is to break down the barriers which make the mind friendly towards only a limited selection of beings to cultivate an all-pervading kindness.

As already stated, most meditation is carried out under the guidance of a specialist meditation master because this practice requires personal guidance for each person. As the master gets to know his pupil on a personal basis, he will then be able to ascertain the level of his development, and thus lead him forward to ever deepening experiences while at the same time guarding him from dangers on the way, particularly the inappropriate use of power that some forms of meditation may produce.

Monks from the Theravada school tend towards the more austere practices of meditating alone, sometimes in forests or cemeteries, so as to more easily attain to a state

of total detachment and disinterest in the world and all of
its entanglements and meaninglessness. These monks
would not eat at all unless someone brought food to them,
but even then they will only eat one meal a day. They
choose only to sleep at night sitting in an upright position
under an umbrella. They wander from place to place for
months at a time, only resorting to temples for shelter
during the rainy season. They often make claim to fantastic
out-of-the-body spiritual experiences and tell of journeys
they have taken in their spirits to other worlds. Claim is
made to various forms of levitation where they apparently
float from place to place, meet and converse in their travels
with all sorts of supernatural angelic beings. Such
experiences would be related to their followers with the
enthusiasm of an evangelist. In Northern Buddhism some
of the more devout monks could spend as much as three
years, three months and three days in total seclusion; they
may choose tiny huts or caves for their meditation.

The Practice of Zen

In Zen, each school has developed an established institution called a 'meditation hall' – a place set apart for
developing the inner life through various means and
postures of meditation. Special platforms called *tan* which
are about eight feet long and three feet high are constructed
at one end of the hall. Each monk will be spaced equally
along the tan and this space will be used for sleeping,
sitting, meditating and anything else permitted in the hall.
A spacious shelf is built in above the tan which is covered
by a curtain, and bedding together with other personal
items are kept hidden on the shelf. There will be schedules
of meditation, with bells being rung at particular times
to remind the faithful – sometimes as early as 3 a.m.
Monks sometimes spend as many as nine hours at a time
alternating between meditation methods, by sitting in the
lotus position on the tan, then walking round and round
a Buddhist image. On occasions for the more serious

devotee, this process of meditation could extend to up to fourteen hours. These exercises are still practised in many temples in South Korea, a Zen training temple in Japan and in Taiwan.

Zen monks interpret the meaning of prayer in terms of 'inner self reflection' rather than asking for help from any outside source. They also engage in *sutra* reading, prayer recitation, incense offering, bowing and expressing their thanks to those 'above' them, such as the Buddhas, Bodhisattvas, masters and teachers. Zen is most often practised in one of two ways. First using the methods of meditation indicated above and second through sharp question/answer exchanges between the master and the pupil.

The narration of *koans* (incomprehensible riddles), together with stories and parables is quite normal. A common expression used in Zen is 'suchness'. This is difficult to define. It probably means 'everything is much the same'; it tries to convey the idea that the down to earth every day events of life are really what existence is all about. 'Suchness' of life is the everyday humdrum of doing ordinary things – but engaging in each one, with equanimity and poise, not cluttered up, by having to follow certain beliefs (dogma), not fettered to whatever claim may hold one. Zen simply says 'Let go. Don't keep trying to keep the unkeepable, hold the unholdable, grasp the ungraspable – be at one with everything, but hold on to nothing.' That is *satori* – salvation.

Whichever branch of Buddhism one explores in terms of their devotional and spiritual activities, behind them all a number of common factors may be seen. One, as indicated above, is to achieve this special category of 'wisdom'. Another equally important goal is to acquire merit for oneself, with the view to escaping from suffering which is caused because of one's personal existence. This is particularly the emphasis of the Theravada school. A further closely linked objective would be to generate merit for other people. These would include the 'living dead' (one's ancestors), those in particular need, even evil doers and finally the community as a whole. This belief is more the emphasis of the Northern Mahayana school. There is generally, the understanding that merit can be gained by one person and transferred or credited to another's 'spiritual bank balance'. This is seen as the key purpose for the Bodhisattvas in the Mahayana schools. A further common goal would be to acquire spiritual power in order to be able to exorcise demons, heal the sick, and find answers for devotees who come with urgent problems, such as 'where exactly are my herd of buffalo – they disappeared into the jungle two weeks ago and I cannot find them?' Through various forms of 'insight' (intuitive knowledge), and 'divination' (gathering knowledge from the spirit world), the monk may be able to accurately locate the buffalo herd. Such 'miracles' raise the credibility and reputation of the monk and strengthen the faith of the devotees.

The Role of Women in Buddhism

While considering the nature of the Sangha and monks, one must not overlook the significance of the role of women. The Buddha himself, perhaps due to family pressure, instituted the order of Bhikkunis, or nuns. The Buddha's stepmother cut off her hair, shaved her head and appearing before him in saffron robes appealed to join the order. It was only after the insistence of Ananda that he acceded because the Buddha is reported to have said that the life of the Buddhist religion would be shortened by 500 years, if women were permitted to join. Women did finally gain admission and the female order of Bhikkunis was founded. For hundreds of years the nuns lived in the same way as men in 'nunneries', but they recognised their subservience to the monks.

In Tantric Buddhism women are honoured because they are regarded as equal with men, but having a different quality. The man is personified or symbolised as *karuna* which means 'compassion', and women are personified as *prajna*, meaning 'perfect wisdom'. There are thousands of images throughout Tibet showing the physical sexual union, which is supposed to symbolise the inner meaning of joining *karuna*, compassion (men) with *prajna* wisdom (women), together. The spiritual meaning is understood to be far more significant than merely a physical union. Certain images of Bodhisattvas (*Kuan-Yin*), are presented as female deities, thus indicating their importance in some Buddhist schools.

In spite of its enthusiastic beginnings, the women's movement declined over the centuries and while there are still thousands of nuns, they are not, so Christmas Humphries indicates, recognised as belonging to the Sangha. In spite of this, the service of the nuns cannot be overestimated in terms of their contribution to Buddhist scholarship, and even more so in their service to humanity. Many of them have come from broken homes or families or have experienced some personal tragedy, so they really do understand the true nature of 'suffering'. It may be because of this that they are so compassionate, engaging in social welfare and caring for people, especially in Sri Lanka, Thailand and Myanmar (Burma).

1. These details can be found in E. Conze (ed.), *Buddhist Scriptures* (Penguin Classics, 1969), pp. 75–77.
2. Jack Kornfield, *Living Buddhist Masters* (Unity Press, 1977).
3. H. W. Schumann, *Buddhism* (Rider & Co., 1973), p. 122.
4. For a more detailed description of these 'states of mind' see Peter Harvey, *An Introduction to Buddhism* (Cambridge University Press, 1990), p. 250.

8

Propagating the Faith – The Missionary Mandate of Buddhism

For hundreds of years Buddhism was virtually unknown in the West. When whispers of such oriental faiths were first heard, they were regarded as remote, mysterious, quaint, perhaps primitive, but certainly not relevant to predominantly Christian countries which would not consider such beliefs as serious or reason-able. Although there may have been occasional contacts with these 'mystery religions' by a few individuals in bygone centuries, the first recorded cultural exchanges between East and West began with Alexander the Great around 300 BC, when his armies spread east as far as India. One can see the effect of Greek art in some of the Buddhist images around this time. The first mention of Buddhism in Christian sources can be found in the writings of Clement of Alexandria in AD 200, when he records 'And there are those in India who follow the commandments of the Buddha, whom they revere as a god because of his immense holiness.'[1] There must have been considerable interaction between Buddhism and Christianity during the first century AD. This would be due to the expansion of the gospel by the apostles of the Nestorian Church, the history of which we in the West are so ignorant, as they spread eastward across the sub-continent of India and further afield as far as Tibet, China and Japan.

It is recorded that Franciscan missionaries met with devout mendicant Buddhist monks at the court of the Mongol Emperor in Peking and they reported back how impressed they were with their devotion. We know that the first Christian missionary to Japan, Francis Xavier, made good friends with a Buddhist abbot there. The story is recorded of a linguistic blunder made by Francis Xavier when he introduced the Latin word for God, *Deus*, pronounced 'Deusu' which to Japanese ears sounded the same as 'the great lie'. This was hardly helpful when he was trying to convey the truth of the gospel to his Buddhist friends, calling it a great lie!

Historically, Christian missionary writings tended to emphasise the advance of Christianity rather than explaining the doctrines of those whom they were trying to convert. There was little explanation or amplification regarding the nature of Buddhism in missionary biography, unless there were anecdotal recordings of local myths and superstitions. This approach linked together with the expansion of Western colonialism meant that Christianity was regarded as a threat. For centuries, little was heard of Buddhism in the West except from the rather bland missionary annals.

It was not until the beginning of the nineteenth century that serious study of Buddhism was undertaken by Western scholars. Under the discipline of Indology (the study of India), it was natural that Buddhism would be one of the subjects for research. Before this stage of development, even such prominent scholars as Schopenhauer (1788–1860) who pioneered Buddhist studies in Germany, apparently had not separated the distinctive doctrinal elements of Buddhism and Hinduism. Eugene Burnouf, a French scholar, has been regarded as the founder of modern Buddhist studies through the publication of the history of Buddhism (1844). The year 1881 was also significant because Hermann Oldenberg published his classic biography of the Buddha's life.

Buddhism in England

It was only towards the end of the nineteenth century, that there was evidence of any wider interest in Buddhism in Britain. The subject had previously been left very much to the concern of learned scholars. A number of events occurred about the same time. A well-known sympathiser of the Buddhist cause, Sir Edwin Arnold, one time editor of the *Daily Telegraph* (1879), following visits to Asia, wrote 'The Light of Asia' a lengthy Victorian poem extolling the virtues of Buddhism. This rather 'romantic' recollection, a comparison and contrast between East and West, appealed to Western sensitivities of the time, ranging from pity for the 'primitive savage' on the one hand to admiration for the 'noble savage' on the other. The poem has been described as 'the most potent evangelist in the literature of Western Buddhism'. It portrayed, in both a 'sympathetic and sentimental style', the Buddha as a figure akin to Jesus Christ. The following are a few verses from this poem:

> I Buddha who wept with all my brothers' tears,
> whose heart was broken by a whole world's woe
> Laugh and am glad, for there is liberty,
> Ho! ye who suffer! Know.

> Ye suffer from yourselves. None else compels,
> None other holds you that ye live and die,
> And whirl upon the wheel, and hug and kiss
> Its spokes of agony,
> Its tire of tears, its nave of nothingness.

> The Dew is on the lotus! – rise, Great Sun!
> And leave my leaf and mix me with the wave,
> *Om mani padme*, *hum*, the Sunrise comes!
> The dewdrop slips into the Shining Sea!

This extract contains the essence of Buddhist faith, namely that Siddhartha Gotama saw and identified with the world of suffering and woe which is the inevitable result of karma – the law of cause and effect. The karma of previous lives dictates the present condition – but we can rejoice for there is a way to leave life's 'spokes of agony', to be absorbed into the Shining Sea!

The production of this poem coincided with the visit of the first Buddhist missionary to Great Britain, *Dharmapala*, who was welcomed by Sir Edwin Arnold, T. W. Rhys Davids, and other devotees. On a subsequent visit *Dharmapala* founded the Maha Bodhi Society (1926) and established a monastery for monks from Sri Lanka.

A certain Alan Bennett McGregor, inspired we are told by 'The Light of Asia', is reported to have been ordained as a Buddhist monk in Burma in 1901. He returned to England in 1907, assumed the name Ananda Metteya and formed a small Buddhist Society. In 1908 Metteya, with three other monks, headed the first Buddhist mission to England. As a result of this visit the Buddhist Society of Great Britain and Ireland was founded with Professor Rhys Davids as President. This was the beginning of a movement which struggled hard for acceptance among English people. Events began to accelerate during this period.

The now famous Dr Suzuki came to Britain in 1936 and spoke on Zen Buddhism at the World Congress of Faiths in London. An important Trade Mission from Tibet came to this country in 1948 and introduced to the market place the mystique of Tantric Buddhism with its emphasis on the exotic and the erotic. The publication of *The Tibetan Book of the Dead*, or 'The After-Death Experiences on the Bardo Plane' according to Lama Kazi Dawa-Samdup's English rendering first published by Oxford University Press in 1927, threw back the veil and enabled Westerners to begin to understand some of the Tibetan tradition, with its preoccupation with 'Thanatology' (the science of death). This book has been called 'The Travellers Guide to Other Worlds'.

Then with the translations of numerous Buddhist texts from Sri Lanka, Thailand, Burma, Nepal and Tibet by various European sages, the European market began to be flooded with Scriptures and commentaries on the Buddhist faith. Thomas Rhys Davids gave his famous Hibbert Lectures on Buddhism and not long after this there emerged the Buddhist (Pali) Text Society, which began to produce prolific translations of the Buddhist Scripture.

The public emergence of Buddhism to the market place in Britain was innovative and surprising. Christmas Humphries reported that a certain J. R. Pain, an ex-soldier from Burma, was seen to be preaching Buddhism from a soap box in London's Hyde Park. The soldier subsequently opened a bookshop in Bury Street for the sale of Buddhist literature.

Hans Küng records that

Buddhist societies, periodicals and important converts all over the world now led to a completely different attitude toward Buddhism and finally to a Buddhist mission (whether promoting classical Buddhism or some contemporary adaptation of Buddhism) in the Americas and Europe. In the twentieth century, both scholarly and popular literature on Buddhism in Europe and America, but also in India, Sri Lanka and Japan has swollen to such proportions that hardly anyone can still keep up with it. And Buddhism itself has received so many impulses for renewal from this research that nowadays the prejudices of the old missionaries (that the Buddhist scriptures are neither published nor read) have become totally obsolete.[2]

It would be no exaggeration to state that during the last thirty years many schools of Buddhism have been enthusiastically engaging in all forms of missionary work in order to expand their cause in the West. With the previous apparent lack of success, Buddhism was now being forced to respond to new challenges and opportunities for cross-cultural style 'evangelism'. Certain schools, in their desire to make Buddhism relevant and popular, began to 'contextualise' the teaching of Buddhism to attract Westerners, by introducing 'Sunday School' style meetings with choruses and hymn singing as part of the routine education process. Organisations such as the Western Buddhist Order (WBO), the World Fellowship of Buddhism (WFB) (1950) and World Buddhist Sangha Council (1966) were established to promote Buddhism in the West and world-wide.

The new approach to other religions of the Roman Catholic Church since Vatican II, indicating that salvation is possible for others who are sincere in their own faiths, together with the 'liberal' emphasis of the World Council of Churches with its emphasis on the vague but popular idea of 'dialogue' with other faiths has encouraged this whole process.

So we see that Buddhism has continued to gain greater popularity, enjoying greater prominence and acceptance within religious debate. Having been launched on to the religious market place of ideas, it was championed not only by a virtually anonymous orator at Speakers' Corner, but by respected intellectual figures such as Christmas Humphries who, as already intimated, together with Alan McGregor, formed a Buddhist Lodge under the auspices of the Theosophical Society. This subsequently seceded from the Theosophical Society and shortly afterwards Humphries became the President of the Buddhist Society in London, a post which he held for forty years.

Christmas Humphries was born in London in 1901, came from a family line of lawyers, was called to the Bar on leaving Cambridge, became Senior Prosecuting Counsel at the Old Bailey and like his father before him sat as circuit Judge between 1968–1976. Humphries founded the Buddhist Society in 1924 which is now the largest Buddhist organisation in Europe. He has written at least six books on Buddhism, the most popular of which is simply called *Buddhism* and is published by Penguin Books.

The most famous 'handbook' published by Humphries was 'The Twelve Principles of Buddhism'.[3] The contents of this single sheet are supposed to encapsulate the essence of Buddhist teaching. It became so popular that it has been translated into at least fourteen languages. The brief text is so definitive and formative that it is considered to be the basis for a future world Buddhism which would hopefully incorporate the three streams of Mahayana, Theravada and Zen into one river – 'a new vehicle of salvation'. Because the fourteen points are so informative and determinative, I reproduce them here:

1. Buddhists are taught to show the same tolerance, forbearance and brotherly love to all men without distinction; and an unswerving kindness towards the members of the animal kingdom.

2. The Universe was evolved, not created, and it functions according to law, not according to the caprice of any God.

3. The truths upon which Buddhism is founded are natural. They have we believe been taught in successive kalpas, or world periods, by certain illuminated beings called Buddhas, the name Buddha meaning 'enlightened'.

4. The fourth teacher in the present kalpa was Sakya Muni, or Gautama Buddha, who was born in a royal family in India about 2,500 years ago. He is an historical personage and his name was Siddhartha Gautama.

5. Sakya Muni taught that ignorance produces desire, unsatisfied desire is the cause of rebirth, and rebirth, the cause of sorrow. To get rid of sorrow, therefore, it is necessary to extinguish desire; and to extinguish desire, it is necessary to destroy ignorance.

6. Ignorance fosters the belief that rebirth is a necessary thing. When ignorance is destroyed the worthlessness of every such rebirth, considered as an end in itself, is perceived, as well as the paramount need of adopting a course of life by which the necessity of such repeated births can be abolished. Ignorance also begets the illusive and illogical idea that there is only one existence for man, and the other illusion that this one life is followed by states of unchangeable pleasure or torment.

7. The dispersion of all this ignorance can be attained by the persevering practice of an all-embracing altruism in conduct, development of intelligence, wisdom in thought, and destruction of desire for the lower personal pleasures.

8. The desire to live being the cause of rebirth, when that is extinguished rebirths cease and the perfected individual attains by meditation that highest state of peace called nirvana.

9. Sakya Muni taught that ignorance can be dispelled and sorrow removed by the knowledge of the four Noble Truths, viz:

1. The miseries of existence.

2. The cause productive of misery, which is the desire ever renewed of satisfying oneself without being able ever to secure that end.

3. The destruction of that desire, or the estranging of oneself from it.

4. The means of obtaining this destruction of desire. The means which he pointed out is called the Noble Eightfold path, viz: Right Belief: Right Thought; Right Speech; Right Action; Right Means of Livelihood; Right Exertion; Right Remembrance; Right Meditation.

10. Right Meditation leads to spiritual enlightenment or the development of that Buddha-like faculty which is latent in every man.

11. The essence of Buddhism as summed up by the Tathagata (Buddha) himself is:

To cease from all sin,

To get virtue,

To purify the heart.

12. The universe is subject to natural causation known as 'karma'. The merits and demerits of being in past existences determine his condition in the present one. Each man therefore, has prepared the cause of the effects which he now experiences.

13. The obstacles to the attainment of good karma may be removed by the observance of the following

precepts, which are embraced in the moral code of Buddhism, vis: 1. Kill not; 2. Steal not; 3. Indulge in no forbidden sexual pleasure; 4. Lie not; 5. Take no intoxicating or stupefying drug or liquor. Five other precepts not here enumerated should be observed by those who would attain more quickly than the average layman the release from this misery and rebirth.

14. Buddhism discourages superstitious credulity. Gautama Buddha taught it to be the duty of a parent to have his child educated in science and literature. He also taught that no one should believe what is spoken by any sage, written in any book, or affirmed by a tradition, unless it accords with reason.[4]

By the time this document had found its way into the market place, there were already the beginnings of other Buddhist organisations in this country. Some schools or branches emerged when in 1954 a Buddhist temple was opened by monks from Sri Lanka at 10 Ovington Gardens, London. This was to be a training centre for Bhikkus of the Theravada School. Then in 1956 a house was rented at 50 Alexandra Road, St John's Wood for the first English temple – it became a home for English members of the order and it was here on English soil that the first full ordination of English monks occurred.

Theravada Buddhism

In 1962 a Canadian named Ananda Bodhi, who trained as a monk in Thailand, founded the Hampstead Buddhist *Vihara* under the auspices of the English Sangha Trust which had been established a few years earlier through the influence of a William Purfhurst who also had gone to Thailand to be ordained. In 1966 developments came to a climax and, with the backing of the Trust, an ornate temple was constructed in Wimbledon, built in classic Thai architectural style. This is now open for all who would follow the Theravada school. It is situated at 14 Calonne Road, Wimbledon, Parkside, London SW19 5JH. Ananda Bhodi then moved on to establish the Johnstone House

Meditation Centre in Dumfriesshire. This has since developed into a centre for the study of Tibetan Buddhism. In 1971 a famous Thai monk, Ajara Cha, moved to England and by 1978 he had formed a Sangha for Western monks. This developed quite rapidly, so that centres were also opened in Northumberland (1981) and Devon (1985).

Tibetan (or Esoteric) Buddhism

Tibetan Buddhism was popularised (again among the student world) in 1970 with a book written by John Blofeld entitled *The Way of Power*.

As a result of regular visits by the Dalai Lama to this country, Tibet has been highly profiled on television programmes. These have centred on the plight of Tibetans, with pictures of Buddhist monks being persecuted, their temples and culture being destroyed. Such images have evoked a great deal of sympathy.

While it is still true to say that the mystery surrounding the Buddhist religion is still ill-defined to most British people, a new climate of interest has arisen. Add strange sounding names from far away places with hints of eroticism, sexual freedom and drugs and you have a recipe that will titillate the attention of young back-packers who think that Khatmandu or Lhasa is just one step away from *Nirvana*, the end of their spiritual journey.

A study centre called the Brighton Buddhist Centre was established for the study of the Tibetan school. It has a publishing house, Wisdom Publications, which is dedicated to producing materials for the propagation of Tibetan Buddhism. There are also plans to establish a college of religious studies. It is recorded that 'there are in the UK alone some sixty-five Tibetan Buddhist centres, dozens of books including significant translations of the Tibetan Buddhist canon and teachings'.[5] The latest centre, the Holy Island Project, aims to purchase the Holy Island off the West Coast of Scotland.

Zen Buddhism

The Nichiren form of Zen has a main centre near Maidenhead where regular lectures are given for devotees. It claims 3000 converts with five regional centres and over a hundred small groups meeting in houses. There is another centre for a different school within Zen in Nacton, Suffolk, popularised by Douglas Harding who discovered, not a 'hole in the head' experience, but literally a 'headless experience' (see below). The now famous Dr D.T. Suzuki from Japan, the primary exponent of Zen, became recognised (in the West) since his visits and because of his famous writings on Zen Buddhism. A British priest Thomas Merton popularised Zen spirituality through a number of books he wrote, principally *On Zen*. This school made a hit in the 1960s with a number of books whose titles were irresistible to the unsatisfied mind of the average young Westerner. Who would not be interested in *Zen and the Art of Motor Cycle Maintenance*? This together with the popularisation of the Eastern martial arts, judo, karate, kung fu and kendo which brought together mastery of the physical and the spiritual, filled a vacuum of emptiness and longing in the lives of aimless Westerners both young and old. On top of all this, a series of films, which led Westerners into new dimensions of the ethereal and mystical, featuring Bruce Lee, did nothing less than usher in a cult following.

But that is still not the end; a certain Douglas Harding, previously mentioned, has made Zen quite popular to enthusiasts in the West by developing a contemporary interpretation on how to discover 'the void nature' or as he calls it 'the headless way', within oneself. Harding is supposed to have become 'enlightened' because of a particular experience he had one day of 'being without a head'. He states concerning this experience:

> It was as if I had been born that instant, brand new, mindless, innocent of all memories . . . it took me no time at all to notice that this nothing, this hole where a head should have been, was no ordinary vacancy, no

mere nothing. On the contrary, it was very much occupied. It was a vast emptiness vastly filled, a nothing that found room for everything – room for grass, trees, shadowy distant hills . . . I had lost a head and gained a world.[6]

The process by which one 'loses one's head' has developed into a particular methodology or 'experimentation' that leads to 'self realisation'. It is so complicated that it is beyond the realms of ordinary people to aspire to. The promised results after becoming 'headless', however, are very attractive . . . freedom from greed, hate, fear and delusion.

While these schools have been developing along their own separate pathways, there were still those who wanted to follow Humphries's ideas of a pan-denominational style of Buddhism. Such idealism has been developed further in England by an organisation called Friends of the World Buddhist Order, which seeks to promote a 'middle way' between the various streams of Buddhism. This is not the only goal of the FWBO. They are also enthusiastic to present Buddhism, sensitively adapted to the taste of the Western palate. An English Buddhist monk named Sangharakshita, who spent twenty years in India practising Buddhism, returned to this country and founded the FWBO in 1967. A fundamental goal of the movement is to assure Westerners that they do not need to become Asian or Indian in order to practise Buddhism, but that it should be effectively enculturated here. They make it very clear what their principles and practices are in an introductory booklet which states that, because of new social and cultural conditions, Buddhism will need to be presented in a new way. They affirm that Westerners will not need to 'cut loose from their own cultural roots to take up Buddhism'. Western art and culture are seen as an aid to personal development within Buddhism to the extent that experiments are engaged upon even to produce Buddhist images 'which are gradually becoming more Western in appearance'.

The FWBO now run nineteen public centres in Britain. These are autonomous communities with no rules; a very appealing prospect to many a disenchanted Westerner. 'As Buddhism does not recognise the existence of a creator god, there are no commandments to obey either.' Having stated this in the booklet, it is then pointed out that members of the order undertake to practise a traditional set of ethical precepts that relate to all actions of body, speech and mind. Upon ordination, a new name from either the Pali or Sanskrit language is given to each new member. Another goal of the FWBO is to encourage members to attain to what is termed 'wholeness'. This is centred on the concept of *mandala* which they interpret as community, this includes the establishing of a public centre with its central focus on the Buddha and Enlightenment. The practice of meditation is central to the whole process, but there are a number of courses offered at the centres that focus on the *Dharma*. This in turn enables a person (as a raft enables one to cross a river) to progress to 'the other shore'. Large country houses have been obtained in various places round the country, including Norfolk, North Wales, Shropshire and a 200-acre wild and beautiful valley called 'The Secret Realm', perched high in the mountains in South East Spain.

Two other initiatives of the FWBO are the establishment of the Windhorse Trading Company which has a turnover of over four million pounds, two hundred thousand pounds of which was channelled in 1994 into social concerns, from aiding children of Tibetan refugees, to helping slum dwellers in India. Proceeds are also used for translation of Buddhist books (Windhorse Publications) into many European languages. A quarterly magazine is also published called *Dharma Life*. This presents the sophisticated, contemporary, attractive face of Buddhism by using the latest publishing techniques. A three-year study course is now offered for *mitras* (an Indian word for 'friends') who wish to have a deepening involvement with the order. Another centre for the sale of a prolific number of books about Buddhism is the Wisdom Book Shop, Hoe Street, London E17, which produces quarterly supplements advertising the latest books on Zen and Tibetan Buddhism, maintaining 'our on-site book shop contains the largest selection of Buddhist books on sale in the UK'. The centre also sells videos and cassettes of famous masters including the Dalai Lama.

Added to all this – if anybody needed proof that Buddhism was enthusiastically engaged in missionary activity – we now find that information is not just available in books, shops or on our doorsteps, but even in our living room – or wherever your personal computer happens to be. You need go no further. Surfing the electronic highway from home will take you into another 'new world'. Among the proliferation of Buddhist Web-sites, you can now visit 'Electronic Bodhidharma', download sound files of the 'Gyuto Tantric Choir' almost *ad infinitum*. *Dharma Life* magazine states 'The cyberspace experience is destined to transform us because it's an external mirror of something that Buddhists have always said, which is that the world we think we see "out there" is an illusion!'[7]

So, 'high-tech' is the name of the game. Surfing the Internet has now become a primary means by which Buddhism is being propagated throughout the world and particularly in this country with literally hundreds of web-sites to drop in on. You can find everything you always wanted to know about Buddhism and not have to read a single book.

It is almost impossible to recount exactly what is going on in the world of Buddhism in Europe today, things are happening so fast. As indicated above, the Dalai Lama is encouraging the purchase of the Holy Island off the West Coast of Scotland 'to foster world peace through the founding of an international inter-faith Centre for Peace, Retreat and Reconciliation'. Application to the Millennium Commission for funding for the purchase of the Island has already been made.

The *Middle Way* journal, published by the Buddhist Society, has at the back a section called 'Newsround'. This details an amazing range of activities of various societies in Britain, from a new Zen temple being opened near

Luton, which is a branch of the Temple of Shobo-an Zen centre in London, to news of a celebration of eighteen years in England of the Tibetan Sakya centre, which has moved to St Andrew's Bristol. There are advertisements for special correspondence courses on basic Buddhism, ten-day *Vipassana* meditation courses at the International Meditation Centre in Wiltshire, various Summer Schools and offers of special holiday journeys 'In the Footsteps of the Buddha – a pilgrimage through India, and Nepal', for 1996 and 1997.

Although numbers are still relatively small, the impact of Buddhism in the market place of ideas is far beyond membership of its various schools. It influences education, business, and is freely offered to those in this rat race of Western living. Techniques to reduce stress and strain which, when Christianity and the peace that Christ offers has been rejected, appear to many to be a viable alternative.

Statistically, the *Buddhist Directory* of 1994 stated that there were at least 130,000 practising Buddhists in this country. The new edition, to be published in 1997, indicates a massive increase (perhaps as many as 300,000), with as many as 350 centres in Britain alone. There are no statistics available to ascertain how many of these are from immigrant communities.

It would not be right to give the impression that everything is so squeaky clean and without blemish in Buddhism, that there are no problems within or between the various schools of belief. This of course is not the case because we are all human, subject to power struggles, jealousies, splits and divisions. These unfortunately do occur between various schools and indeed within some schools. While it is not right to dwell on such weaknesses, it is only fair to paint a true picture, 'warts and all'. There are 'theological' struggles and personality struggles in Buddhism as anywhere else. For example, for many years in Tibetan Buddhism for instance, there has been an on-going theological battle concerning the recognition of one particular deity *Dorje Shugden*, who is purported to be the *Dharma* protector. Behind this theological difference, there have been political struggles and the emergence of a school called the New Kadampa Tradition which has been set up to 'protect' the protector deity. The Dalai Lama has been brought into the debate and has declined to undertake the practice of *Dorje Shugden* – 'The Dalai Lama as both a political and a spiritual figure considers that this practice is not skilful or suitable for the present situation of Tibetan people or Tibetan Buddhism in the world.'[8]

Conclusion

One may well ask the question why does Buddhism have such a growing attraction to people in the West? There are a number of self-evident answers to this question. It offers a number of trendy 'up-beat' attractive alternatives in comparison with what is justifiably regarded as a decadent Western culture, with its breakdown of cohesive family life, immorality, injustice, disregard for the environment, individualism and the perceived irrelevance of 'down-beat' Christianity. There is a strong sense of community within the Sangha which many see as an agreeable alternative for broken down family life. There are expected set boundaries of behaviour, which give a sense of direction, well being and security. There are 'ideal' goals to which the whole community aspires. There are common concerns to improve the environment, in terms of ecology, and morality. Perhaps more than anything else, Buddhism offers a viable lifestyle which does not have to be preoccupied with the everyday humdrum of home and business affairs of the average nine-to-five person in Britain. This belief system questions the obsessive preoccupation of Western people with self-centred materialism, and offers an attractive 'middle path'. The disenchanted, those looking for alternative lifestyles, the new agers, the road travellers, the back packers and the 'down to earth' people concerned for issues not being dealt with by the government; the 'philosophers', in fact all who are dissatisfied with the usual pat answers they are given (which are not answers), will find much of what Buddhism has to offer an alternative attraction.

This is not to say that genuine Christianity does not have all of this and more to offer; it is to say that most people in Britain and Europe, have been, for so long, innoculated with a misrepresentation of the gospel and have therefore become immune and unresponsive to its 'good news'.

1. Clement of Alexandria 1.15, see John Ferguson, *Clement of Alexandria* (Twayne Publishers, 1974), p. 15.
2. Hans Küng, *Christianity and the World Religions* (SCM Press, 1986), p. 309.
3. While some attribute the authorship to Humphries, others state that it was Colonel H. S. Olcott, one of the founding presidents of the Theosophical Society, who proposed this 'common platform' for all Buddhists.
4. Christmas Humphries, *Buddhism* (Penguin Books, 1951), pp. 71–73.
5. *The Middle Way*, May 1966, Vol. 71, No. 1, p. 12.
6. Ann Bancroft, *Religions of the East* (Heinemann, 1974), p. 177.
7. FWBO web page is hhtp://www.fwbo.org. For all Tibetan Buddhist schools see http://www.tibet.org.
8. *The Middle Way*, August 1966, Vol. 71, No. 2, p. 132.

Suggestions for Further Reading

The following list of books is suggested as a guideline for those desiring to study further, they are quoted from in this book, but do not represent all the books referred to.

Bancroft A., *Religions of the East* (London: Heinemann, 1974).
This book is especially helpful because it links Buddhism to its roots in Hinduism and Jainism. It is well written and illustrated. The reader looking for an understanding of all religions will find this very useful.

Burnett, David, *The Spirit of Buddhism – A Christian Perspective on Buddhist Thought* (Crowborough Sussex: Monarch Books, 1966).
This book covers in sufficient detail most Buddhist Doctrines and beliefs, it seeks to view and interpret them dispassionately from a Christian perspective.

Harvey, Peter, *An Introduction to Buddhism: Teachings, History and Practices* (Cambridge: Cambridge University Press, 1990).
Presents a comprehensive survey of Buddhism in general and offers an introduction to all the schools of Buddhism. It seeks to explore the functions and practices of the religion and is helpful for the person who desires to gain general knowledge of the whole range of beliefs within the various schools.

Humphries, C., *The Buddhist Way of Life* (London: Allen & Unwin, 1969).
This is perhaps the most concise and easy to read scholarly presentation of the essence of Buddhism, by its most renowned English disciple.

Pye, Michael, *The Buddha*, (London: Duckworth, 1979).
Centres around the two great legends of the Buddha's enlightenment and Nirvana. A shorter book, well written and focused particularly on the Buddha as a person.

Rahula, W., *What the Buddha Taught* (Bedford: Gordon Fraser Gallery, 1967).
This is the seventh book written by the well-known scholar from Sri Lanka on Buddhism. As its title indicates it focuses particularly on the teaching of the Buddha 'everything which is commonly accepted as the essential and fundamental teaching of the Buddha'. Chapter 8 is particularly helpful where the author applies the *Dharma* to modern life today.

Saddhatissa, H., *The Buddha's Way* (London: George Allen & Unwin, 1971).
This book is chosen for two reasons. It is one of the two listed written in English by a non-Western scholar. The preface states that while numerous books have been written on Buddhism, none has really answered the call for a straightforward approach to the *Dharma* of a non-scholastic nature. The book is especially useful for the material in the appendices. The chronological Table of Events in East and West up till 1968 is helpful.

Thomas, Edward, *The Life of Buddha as Legend and History* (London: Routledge & Kegan Paul, 1975).
This is rather specialist in that it attempts to sort out the difference between the Buddha as myth and the Buddha as history. There is a useful appendix on the Theravada Scriptures, but there is little reference to expansion of Buddhism or its contemporary relevance.

For further information re Buddhist activities in England contact: The Buddhist Society, 58 Eccleston Square, London SW1V 1PH. *The Buddhist Directory* to be re-printed in 1997 lists almost all activities and centres in British Isles. The UK Christian Centre for Buddhist Studies, PO Box 74, Loughborough, Leics LE11 2ZU was established to encourage dialogue, teach and inform Christians by comparing and contrasting the two beliefs. It seeks to promote an understanding of Buddhism from a Christian point of view.

Index

Ananda, disciple nephew of
    Buddha 17, 23, 28, 29
  green issues 122
anatta (no personhood) 31,
    56, 80
  atman (selfhood) 58
  negative aspects of 81
  no self or soul 92
Asoka (King) 20, 33–5
  history of 20
  teaching 33
  visited Buddha's
    birthplace 114
atman (personhood) 13
avija (ignorance) 15, 66, 77,
    94
  see also ignorance

Boddhisattva 17, 60, 79
  concept of Saviour 135
  one who is dependable
    84
  suffering for others 83
  transference of merit 110
  vow 113
Brahmins 4, 10, 19
Buddha (*budh*) 1

biography 155
birth 2, 4–6, 21, 114
Christ, akin to 156
Christ, comparison with
    79–80
death 19, 28
deification 60
early travels 24–7
enlightenment 12–14, 93
family 3
father: Shuddhodanna 3
footprint 116
Gautama (Gotoma) 2–3,
    160
influence of former beliefs
    12
rebirths, former 4, 12–13
renunciation 8–11
reverencing 110
revulsion at life style 7
Sakiya tribe (Buddha's
    family clan) 5
sermon, first 15
son: Rahula 7–8
temptation 14,
upbringing 6–8
wife: Maya, 5, 21, 25

Buddhism (various schools)
34–45, 64–5, 139
  Britain, development in
162
  contextualising 158
  doctrinal differences 99
  man, view of 75
  missionary movement
34–7, 48, 154–9
  popular Folk Buddhism,
demons and ancestors
130
  scholarship in 146
  theological struggles 168
  Tibetan (Lamaism) 40–2
  Twelve Principles of 159
  Web-sites 167
  West, cultural adaptation
to 165
  West, previously unknown
in 154
*Buddhist Directory for Great
Britain* 168
Buddhist Society of Great
Britain 157

centres in Britain 163, 167–8
  Buddhist Society 172
  Christian Centre for
Buddhist Studies 173
  Holy Island, purchase of
167
  Web-sites 170
  Windhorse Trading
Company 166
Christ, Jesus 12, 17
  comparison between

Christ and Buddha 70,
79–80, 136, 156
Christianity 75, 80–2, 90,
103
councils 29
  Pataliputta (third) 32
  Rajagha (first) 29
  Vesali (second) 31
creation 27, 105
  absence of Creator 15, 94

Dalai Lama 41–3
  death, upon 42
  exiled 128
  new, selection of 106
  West, regular visits to 163
  see also Tibetan Buddhism
desire 99
  destruction of 161
  hindrances, five 148
  wisdom unachievable?
100
Dharma 19, 30, 53, 78, 99
  84,000 sections in 34
  adhering to 119
  commentaries on 34
  conditioned 147
  demise of 30
  eternal wheel of 117
  guide 138
  is of itself redemptive? 137
  issues, application to
contemporary 123
  reading of 110
  taking refuge in 137
  worship centred round
110

Dharma Life magazine 123
discipline 131
   Buddha's austerity 10
   detachment, leading to 150
doha (sin)
   dukkha, contrast to 76
   slave to 81
dukkha see suffering

Eightfold Path 12–14, 119
   deliverance, leads to 78
   destruction of desire by
      161
   environmental issues,
      principles applied to
      123
enlightenment 83, 94
   Bo Tree, under 11
   Christian conversion,
      wrongly used to
      explain 94
   definition of 16
   truths of, three 94
   visiting the place of 115
   women, possibility for
      30

family moral issues 131
   prayers for 113
   role of husband and wife
      132
Folk Buddhism
   demons and ancestors 130
   hope in 96
   scholarship in 146
Friends of the World
   Buddhist Order 165

Britain, centres run in 166
   magazine 166

Hinduism 3, 4, 6, 7
   Scriptures/*Vedas* 6
   transmigration of souls 56
Humphries, Christmas 20,
      45, 83, 88, 89, 94, 118,
      134, 135, 153, 159

ignorance *(avija)* 66
   Emancipation from 94
   suffering, as the cause of
      77

Jataka stories 8, 24, 26, 53,
      85
   depictions of in temple
      decor 141
   miracles 14
   sermons, use in 145
journals
   The Middle Way 167
   Dharma Life 166
   Buddhist Directory 168

Karma (merit) 13, 74, 86–93,
      161
   and AIDS 127
   and laziness 133
   and suffering 128–9
   Damocles sword of 135
   previous lives of 157

'Light of Asia' poem 156,
      157
lotus flower 100–1

Lotus Sutra 32, 47, 48, 59
  Zen, used in 107

Mahayana 17, 49
  5,000 volumes 61
  Asia, expansion across 38
  'Greater Vehicle' 31
  language, chanting in
      original 111
  origin of 37
  salvation for all 37
  schools, comparison
      between 39, 83
mantra (chant) 40, 107
Mara (Satan) 14
meditation 146–50
  aid to: *mantras*/rosaries
      107
  corpse, on 103, 105
  mandala 'Wheel of Life'
      108
  samati method 105
  wipassana method 77,
      105
merit making 110, 132
  temple attendance, value
      of 144
  transference of 66, 92, 93
  giving away of 113
  parents, gaining merit for
      131
  see also Karma
Metteya (Saviour figure) 17,
      18, 19
missionary nature of
      Buddhism 34–7, 48
monks 125, 135–46

Peking, at the court of
      Mongol Emperor in
      154
British, first ordination of
      162
moral issues
  animal welfare 128–9
  Eightfold Path 119
  environmental issues 122
  ethics 127, 128
  family 131
  homosexuality 121
  political issues 126, 142
  precepts 125
  working immorally 121

Nirvana 10, 38, 60, 93–7
  entrance into, postponing
      79, 83
nuns
  enlightened, could be 30
  Sangha, joining the 30,
      117
  see also women

Pali Scriptures 3, 51–8
  reliability 20
  translations of 61
  vocabulary comparison
      with Sanskrit 51
Pali and Sanskrit
  memorisation 145
  origins, meaning and use
      51
  translations 61
pilgrimages 28, 114–6
political issues 126, 142

precepts (regulations) 125
    227 rules 117, 139, 142,
        162
    commandments, ten 138
prophecy 18, 82
    birth of Buddha 82
    Saviour figure 17–18
Pure Land Buddhism 65

Queen Srisuriyotha of
        Thailand 85

reincarnation 31, 74, 134
    500 reincarnations of
        Buddha 78
    animal ascending to
        humanhood 90
    evolution of, endless 79
    rebirth 81, 92
    rebirth, not
        transmigration 56

Sakiya tribe (Buddha's family
        clan) 5
samsara (cycle) 13, 83
Sangha 25, 30
    community, strong sense
        of 169
    expulsion from 143
    nature of, non-political 140
    organisation of 139
    origins of 27
    refuge, taking in 137
Sanskrit 2, 51, 61
Saviour 137
    no God, no Saviour 89
    no external refuge 118

Scriptures 51–5
    Chinese versions 63
    Gems, three (baskets) 54
    Hindu Vedas 6
    Mahayana 59–64
    Tibetan Canon 62–3
    transmission, oral 52
    written down first 20, 35
self (anatta) (self-centred)
        80–1
skandhas (five elements) 31,
        54–8
spirituality 99–102
    Christian perspective 105
    Puja (worship) 111
stupas (relics) 140
    Buddha's birthplace 114
    Buddha's hair (relic) 116
    Buddha's remains shared
        19
    Buddha's tooth (relic) 116
    contents disappear 29
    ten erected 28
substitution (death in place
        of) 83–6, 135
    (merit in place of) 92
suffering (dukkha) 69–72,
        75–8
    and Sin 75
    aspects of 137
    difference between
        Christ and Buddha 70
    fact and effect of 15
    mechanisms, escape 71
    nature of 136
    root cause 81–3
    sin, relation to 69

Temple
  Life 140–3
  buildings, description of
    141
Theravada Buddhism (the
    lesser vehicle) 35, 52
  Bodhisattvas, no 83
  boys in priesthood 92,
    131
  history and development
    34–8
  origins of 31
  'path consciousness' 106
  Sri Lanka, moved to 34
Three Gems, the Buddha, the
    Dharma and the
    Sangha 112, 137
  formula 138
  themes, central 54
  virtue of 144
Tibetan Buddhism
  86 volumes of
    commentary 63
  Book of the Dead 40, 157
  mandala wheel of life 108
  popularised in West 163
  ritual, scape-goat 84
  Shaktiism (eroticism) 106
  Tibetan *Tantras* 62
  see also Dalai Lama
Truths, Four Noble 13, 54
  definition of 72–3

Vajrayana Buddhism
  origin and development
    40
  spread of 39

wipassana (meditation) 77,
    105
women 131–2
  enlightenment possible 30
  family 113
  joining the Sangha as nuns
    30
  nuns 153
  nuns, abstinence from
    sexual intercourse 117
  role of 152
  wife, role of 132
worship
  aids to 107
  confession, no forgiveness
    112
  corporate worship 110
  monks invited to lead at
    home 114
  nature of 109
  Puja, sevenfold devotion
    111
  yantras and *mantras* 67

Yoga
  positions, correct bodily
    101

Zen Buddhism
  'being without a head'
    165
  books on 164
  centres in the West 164
  description of 46
  Koans function and
    meaning 44, 45, 151
  meditation, extended 150

Merton, Thomas, *On Zen* 45
missionary zeal 48–9
Nichiren Shosu 47, 48
origins of 42
practice of 44, 150
Pure Land Buddhism 46

satori (salvation) 43, 45, 151
schools of 45
Soka Gakkai 39, 47
Suzuki, Dr, greatest authority 45